To Russia with Love

To Russia with Love

CHANGING THE LIVES OF ABANDONED CHILDREN

DEBBIE DEEGAN

with Emily Hourican

MERCIER PRESS

IRISH PUBLISHER – IRISH STORY

MERCIER PRESS

Cork

www.mercierpress.ie

© Text: Debbie Deegan, 2012

© Foreword: Marian Keyes, 2012

ISBN: 978 1 78117 038 0

10 9 8 7 6 5 4 3 2

A CIP record for this title is available from the British Library

Printed and bound in the EU.

CONTENTS

FOREWORD BY MARIAN KEYES 7

PREFACE 11

PROLOGUE 18

1 PAPA? 21

2 I WILL COME BACK 37

3 I DON'T WORK WITH DUMB BLONDES 50

4 THE WIZARD OF OZ 64

5 GUARDIAN ANGELS AND MEN OF IRON 76

6 OF FUND-RAISING AND EXTORTION 96

7 YOU CAN GO FOR A WALK, BUT BE BACK IN TEN MINUTES! 108

8 SO MANY STORIES 118

9 THE ONES WE COULDN'T SAVE 136

10 JOE DUFFY, BARRETSTOWN AND BESLAN 149

11 ADOPTIONS AND THE FACEBOOK ERA 163

12 HORTOLOVA – A FAMILY AFFAIR 174

13 SOULMATES 182

14 RUSSIA'S OPRAH, AND AFTER 188

15 WHERE TO NOW? 203

16 FALLING IN LOVE, WITH A FAMILY 219

APPENDIX A: THE PROGRAMMES THAT CHANGED THEIR LIVES 231

APPENDIX B: CASE STUDIES 243

ACKNOWLEDGEMENTS 249

FOREWORD

MARIAN KEYES

Okay, imagine you're an ordinary Dublin housewife, we'll call you Debbie, Debbie Deegan. And imagine that sixteen years ago you took two Russian orphans into your home for a month for a holiday. And imagine that you became completely besotted with the two little girls and couldn't bear the thought of sending them home. And imagine that one of the little girls contracted meningitis and was too sick to travel, but the other little girl wasn't so lucky – no meningitis for her – and had to go back.

And imagine that you were so tormented by your adopted daughter's memories of her former classmates, that you decided to go to Russia to find them, and all your friends and family told you you were a big eejit and to cop on to yourself. And imagine that you didn't speak a word of Russian but you flew to Minsk in the winter, persuaded someone to drive you and eventually found the orphanage, in Hortolova, eight hours south of Moscow.

And imagine that it was worse than your worst nightmares – filthy, stinking, crumbling, with broken, damaged children running around in the middle of winter with no shoes on their

7

feet – and that you were carried out of there a complete basket case.

And imagine that when you got back to Ireland, your friends and family said, 'See, didn't we tell you you were a big eejit', and you replied, 'Shut up, I'm holding a fund-raising coffee morning, get baking.' And imagine that instead of the usual £4.73, you raised £7,000 and all of a sudden you'd founded To Russia With Love.

* * *

With head-spinning speed Debbie found herself sitting down with architects and finding people in Russia who could supervise the rebuilding of an orphanage that housed 150 orphans. (I can't tell you how much this fills me with awe. When my boiler breaks and I've to get a plumber, I'd rather tear off my own head and eat it than have to listen to all the reasons why my boiler can't be fixed and why I need a brand new expensive one instead.)

Her plan had been a quick in-and-out, to make everything shiny and modern and new, then she could walk away and slot back nicely into her old life, almost as if nothing had happened. But then she fell in love ... with the children. 150 children. 150 individuals. 150 human beings, some clever, some cute, some funny, some sporty, some geeky. As diverse and unique as all people are – except that they shared one thing, they had all been denied love, security, safety and any sort of childhood. They were all damaged, but even the most well-adjusted of the children – obviously some human beings are just innately better at survival than others – were desperate for love and affection. And it was then that Debbie understood the real reason fate had brought her to this place – the actual bricks and mortar of the orphanage were almost incidental, she'd been brought there to love the children better.

After I became patron of the charity, I braced myself to visit the orphanage and I might as well tell you, I was dreading it. I thought the accumulated weight of all their sad stories would kill me. But first impressions were hopeful. Since the rebuilding, the orphanage isn't one big, gloomy, Dickensian edifice any longer, but a series of charming wooden houses built in a circle. The bedrooms – only two to three kids to a room – are cheery and colourful. But there's no getting away from the fact that these kids are in this place because terrible things have happened to them.

Many of them come from places of horrific violence. And many – oh so many of them – have been abandoned emotionally, if not actually, by their parents' alcoholism. (Lots of the kids still have a parent who is alive, but they're 'social' orphans, in that the parent isn't fit to take care of them.) Because of this I'd expected the children might be difficult, bratty, withdrawn – who could blame them considering what they've already endured in their short lives? But they were variously charming, polite, mischievous, earnest, sweet, thoughtful, affectionate and above all – and most moving – dignified. I couldn't get over it.

And it's entirely down to Debbie and her team that even though there are 200 children in Hortolova, they're all treated like individuals, just as they would be in a family. I was very moved by the myriad humane little touches, the thoughtfulness, the treats – like taking a load of the lads to Moscow for the Russia versus Ireland match. Or like giving children choices – most orphans have no say in what they eat, what they wear, where they sleep: they get what they get and they can like it or lump it. But Hortolova children are brought to the market and allowed to pick out their own clothes. Mind you, when this first started the children were so paralysed by lack of practice that the market visits took forever.

Ten years after Debbie first became involved, five children from the orphanage went to university. When you think of what they came from, when you think of what their lives were like before Debbie, this is nothing short of a miracle.

Today, Debbie and To Russia With Love (with the support of the Russian authorities) work in each of the twelve orphanages in the region of Bryansk and have literally transformed the lives of thousands of children in the last fourteen years.

PREFACE

I am dedicating this book to the mothers of all our beautiful children, who for many reasons had to abandon their precious children to our care. You missed the joys we experienced, the pride we felt as we watched them grow, graduate, succeed and spread their damaged wings. You could not be there for every Last Bell,* and so we soaked up your children's tears on that day every year. You could not be there as we collected your little ones' bodies from morgues and placed our flowers on their coffins. You could not be there as we watched them write their first Valentine cards, fall in love, get married. You could not be there when we delivered their babies, nursed wounds and taught them to be mums and dads, as they had no idea how to do this. You could not be there when we found their lost brothers and sisters and tried to keep families together. You could not be there when desirables, and undesirables, took your children to foster homes. You could not be there when your little ones asked us to tuck them up, told us about you and asked us to kiss them goodnight. You could not be there when your children scored goals, won dance competitions, skied to gold medals and raced marathons, but we were. We try to be there for everything.

So to all those tragic, lost, broken mothers, we thank you for the honour and for the joy your children give us every day. Until you are able to mind them yourselves, we are honoured to do it for you.

The main protagonists, in no particular order:

Mick Deegan – husband, best friend, loyal supporter, endless funder of me

Monny – world's best mother, an angel to many in Ireland and Russia

Daddy – for passing on the fire-fighting gene and minding our dogs, Fudge and Fifi

Ann Deegan – wonderful grandmother and mother-in-law, made my journeys easier

Trisha McGrath – right arm, loyal friend, travelling companion, guardian angel

Sophie, Zina and Mikey – my three beautiful children. They made it all easy for me, became friends to many and tidied up when I was exhausted

Igor Stepanov – dear friend, minder, adviser, organiser extraordinaire, bodyguard, driver, my Russian voice

Olga Stepanova – beautiful wife of Igor, friend, supporter, currently programmes' manager and our single mums' guardian angel

Ger Ashmore – hygiene-auditor of awful places, loyal friend, guardian angel to many

Noreen Lyons – coordinator of our sponsor families, Trojan worker to this very day

Fergus Lyons – the amazing man behind Noreen and her spreadsheets

Éamonn Lonergan – a very special Irish man and a role model to our boys

Emma Gunne – a wonderful young social worker, who took on a difficult little girl and still cares for her to this day

Joe Bell – original MC of our glittering balls, until replaced by Brendan O'Connor. Friend, loyal supporter and fund-raiser

Vyvienne Bell – the woman behind Joe, host of my return dinners after every trip, loyal fund-raiser

Valya Slizovskya – beautiful mother to sweet Emily, her three-year-old daughter

Fergal McGrath – painfully transparent accountant, ruthless with us all, loyal supporter

Marion Kilbride – networker extraordinaire, fund-raiser, guardian angel to many

Dermot Hearne – wonderful supporter, spectacular Santa, best designer of all things child-friendly

Dr Mark Wheeler – very caring doctor to hundreds of lucky children, saxophone player, singer, fund-raiser, friend

John Mulligan – ethical, strict mentor, expert, philanthropist, author, teacher, bodyguard, close friend, song-writer

Derek Tracy – friend, therapist, civil servant, institution expert, systems genius, tireless worker, lover of all things Russian, painfully positive mentor, travelling companion and poet

Máirtín Ó Dubhghaill – one of the kindest men I have ever met, a father figure to hundreds, guitar player, fund-raiser extraordinaire, a dear friend

Pauline and Gordon Dooley (another wonderful Santa) – kind, generous, loyal supporters, minders of many, fund-raisers

Mary O'Sullivan – writer of many stories, travelling companion, fund-raiser, loyal friend, adviser

Eugene Garrihy and John O'Brien – project managers, humanitarians, loyal friends, changers of children's lives in many places

Noel Quinn – Irish/Moscow builder, supporter, fund-raiser, project manager, guardian angel

Caroline Mahon – initial travelling companion, mentor, adviser, guardian of some very special boys

Brendan O'Connor – journalist, TV presenter, tough on the outside and marshmallow inside, MC, fund-raiser, rescuer, loyal supporter and friend

Grainne Lee – best friend, therapist, psychologist for me, listener, adviser, important letter writer

Adrian McCarthy and Louise Wadley – documentary makers, friends, loyal supporters

Barry Egan – journalist, social diarist, gatherer of auction prizes for fourteen years, loyal supporter, friend

Brenda O'Connell – head of the ball committee, fund-raiser, event expert, friend, adviser, loyal supporter of To Russia With Love; helped by Martina, Catherine, Anne and Carol – all wonderful women who have contributed hugely over the years

Lena Ivanova – translator, model, friend, carer, photographer, loyal supporter

Vlad Ivanov – Lena's lovely husband, one of our first carers

Jerome Westbrooks – my son's basketball coach, personal friend, then coach to our Russian children, fund-raiser, carer, teacher, incredible human, the first African-American into a Russian forest

John Masterson – the one who makes me look good in the papers, makes me say the right things when I don't want to, struggles to fill his day when I'm travelling

Rory and Miriam O'Callaghan – founding members, great people, fund-raisers

Susan O'Sullivan – organiser of ladies lunches, assisted by Carol and Marion

Sveta Loutina – the original brain running the To Russia With Love office

Kevin Oliver – board member, adviser, mentor

Joe and Chris Morton – fund-raisers, loyal supporters

Paula O'Dwyer – board member, adviser, fund-raiser, education adviser, ambulance driver

Zhenya Chevrenenko – dedicated staff member, guardian angel to hundreds, adviser to many, programme manager

Oleg Gordeyev – doctor, friend, loyal supporter of To Russia With Love

Governor Lodkin – supporter, award giver, instrumental in the initial success of To Russia With Love

Governor Denin – great supporter of To Russia With Love and the Irish, a wonderful friend in a high place

Tatyanna Gruzenciva – head of the Department of Education, inspirational, stern adviser, very big boss, friend

Valentine Baleyev – a unique man, a brilliant translator, godfather to Zina

John Patchell – an incredible man who did a great job changing the direction of many children's lives

Maria Campbell – a great girl who went out for three months and stayed for two years; a mother to many to this day

Marina Knoroz – chief psychologist, inspirational, caring friend of the Irish

Uri Ivanov – my dear friend from the Federal Security Bureau (FSB, formerly known as KGB), minder, sadly missed by us all

---

* This is a child's graduation from school. In regular schools, it is a huge event, with the halls decorated and parents crying tears of pride. In an orphanage, although the children have written to invite their parents, they never come. Only the carers are there. For this reason, we never miss it. The children are terrified at what comes next for them. They are leaving the orphanage for the first time and the outside world seems a hostile place. The actual bell is carried by the smallest junior infant girl, on the shoulders of the biggest graduating boy. She rings the bell as the graduates exit the hall. Along with First Bell, the day the junior infants start for the first time, this is the biggest event in Russian family lives.

PROLOGUE

A Tale of Two Promises

This is a tale of two promises. A promise to one little girl that I wouldn't forget her classmates – the children she had grown up with in the orphanage where she had spent her early years – and a promise to another little girl, who had never been hugged before, that I would come back to her orphanage and hug and kiss her on her birthday.

Before I begin, I should say that I love Russia and its people. I have seen many positive changes since my first visit. However, back when we began in 1998, the orphanage, Hortolova, in western Russia, was a deeply shocking experience for a middle-class housewife from Clontarf. It was dark, dirty, abandoned and freezing cold, with broken window panes and no central heating, no working toilets. Situated in the middle of a forest, it was very hard to find, with strange, scruffy old men creeping around the place; they appeared to be using the orphanage as a short-cut to their villages. No one, as far as I could then see, was actually responsible for the children and I was bowled over by how unprotected they were. In retrospect, I can't believe how shallow and western I was in my thinking

– I had wanted to swoop in, bring the children a few sweets, tell them that Zina, their classmate and my adopted daughter, was okay and swoop out. That, I thought, would be the end of it. I'd go back to my nice life, Zina would be able to send a few letters later on if she liked and everything would carry on as normal.

As it turned out, I found myself making a promise to come back. It's a promise that I have repeated again and again, a promise I can't get out of, because these children still have nobody else, no one to fight their corner, to love them, to believe in them. No one to cheer them on when they graduate from the orphanage, to help them prepare for life in an outside world that is terrifying to children who have never had to choose their own clothes or between two types of soup, let alone make any important decisions. Without us, and the wonderful Russian friends we have made on our journey, these children would once again be the forgotten, abandoned, frightened orphans I found on that first, life-changing, trip to Russia.

And no, I have never regretted those promises. Not when I was hauled out of my bed in a cheap Russian hotel in the middle of the night and brought before a gang of thugs who demanded I give them a substantial chunk of the money I had raised in Ireland to help these children. Not when my marriage looked like it wouldn't survive the amount of time and energy I was expending on the charity. Not during all my dealings with Russian bureaucrats who insisted that the children couldn't have their hair washed twice a week because they were only entitled to 2 mls of shampoo each, according to regulations laid down God knows when. Not during any of the difficult, harrowing, frustrating but exhilarating years since I first founded To Russia With Love, even though I have cried myself sick over the unsustainability of it all many times. However, when I look at what we have achieved I can only feel an immense sense of pride and in some cases awe at the staggering numbers involved. The first fourteen years can be summed up as follows:

1.7 million kilometres

5,000 children

€6 million fund-raised

576 Irish volunteers

4 funerals

1 serious car crash

28 lost suitcases

14 Russian 'grandchildren'

17 humanitarian awards

Zero resignations

1

PAPA?

I had been a stay-at-home mum for four years by the time I saw an ad in the newspaper for a meeting to be held for Irish parents to discuss bringing in a group of orphans from Chernobyl. Now of course, I know that not all the children were actually from Chernobyl, which is in Ukraine, but the organisation involved in bringing them over knew well that Chernobyl was a name people would recognise, an emotive word, a label that would guarantee a generous response.

At the time, we were told that by taking the children in for a summer, feeding them, caring for them and letting them breathe fresh air, you gave them two extra years of life. That's far too simplistic, but we believed it. Mick and I had a nice house in Clontarf with plenty of bedrooms. I was at home all day and I was happy to take on anything that was thrown at me. We were on one salary and we weren't wealthy, but I could afford to stay at home and we could just about pay our bills. Frankly, I was probably getting bored – I had wanted to be at the gates every afternoon to collect Sophie, my daughter, when she started school, because my mother had always been there for me – but I also need a lot of stimulation and I was ready for something else. Even now, I always feel I have the capacity to do more in my day. No matter what kind of bedlam is going on around me, I almost never feel panicked or overwhelmed by the volume of things to do. I love lists. The longer the better.

Mikey, my youngest, was at playschool in the mornings, so I was free then, and I had begun to fund-raise for various causes by having coffee mornings at home. In fact, a lot of my friends were just like me – school-gate mums with a bit of spare time (these were the women who later made up my board of directors and are among my best friends to this day); we were a kind of coffee morning brigade, forever doing good for one cause or another. I cringe saying that now, but I also look back on those days with something like regret! We had the luxury of so much time and freedom, if only we'd realised it.

My husband, Mick, and I decided to take two little girls, Zina and Valya, both seven years old, for the summer of 1996. The little Russian girls arrived and we went to the airport to collect them – tiny, undernourished little things, with head lice and threadbare clothes. We put them in the back of the car and they were clearly exhausted. On the way home, Zina leaned forward, put her hand on Mick's shoulder and asked,

'Papa?' And that was it. From that moment, although we didn't discuss it immediately, we both knew that we would keep her, had to keep her. We had never intended to adopt a child, but somehow, when Zina asked that question, the answer became yes.

We had a bedroom ready for the girls, with pink Barbie slippers, pink dressing-gowns, pink pyjamas, everything, and the next day we put them in the bath and started head lice treatment. They were both tiny and skinny; Zina had huge, painful boils on her bum and Valya had worryingly low energy levels, so bad that her lips were purple. Those physical indicators of their lives in the orphanage were awful, but the psychological impact was much harder to address. For example, no matter how many times we showed them the bowl of fruit in the middle of the table, or how to open the fridge, telling them to help themselves if they were hungry (we had learned a few, very basic Russian phrases), they couldn't do it. They just didn't understand the concept. Children in orphanages never see a fridge – food just arrives at mealtimes. And they don't help themselves. All their food is handed to them and they eat what they are given, and that's it. To them, helping themselves felt like stealing.

In Russia so-called 'orphans' often have parents, at least one, maybe two. The problem is their parents are unable, or unwilling, to cope with them. They have problems with alcohol, or crime, or often both. They aren't capable of tending to their children and so they dump them, or the children are removed by the state for their own safety. Sometimes, and this is something I still find incredibly hard to believe, a woman will marry a new husband and one of his conditions will be that he will not raise another man's children. If she chooses him, the children will be abandoned; brought to an orphanage and left there. Usually, the mothers don't come back and visit. They may write once or twice, but rarely much more than that. They almost never feature in their children's lives again. As a result, the trauma suffered by nearly all the children is extreme. They have been abandoned or removed by the police, often after early lives that have been chaotic, squalid and violent. No wonder they have problems with trust. It is heartbreaking, and to this day I still cannot understand it. I have had it explained to me many times by Russians, as far as any explanation is possible – they say that one legacy of communism was that people genuinely believed the state would do a better job – but I can't and don't understand how any mother can walk away from her children.

Zina herself had been in an orphanage since the age of eighteen months, because her birth mother wasn't fit to look after her. Her parents were married, but her father later died, although it seems he did visit Zina once when she was small. She remembers a man wearing a red scarf coming to see her.

One visit may seem pathetically inadequate to us, but it is one more than many Russian 'orphans' get, and for that one visit, Zina was always prepared to love the idea of this man she never knew. For a long time we wondered was this memory of Zina's accurate, or was she perhaps transposing something else to give herself the kind of narrative she so badly wanted, but eventually we found out that she was right, he had visited once. How we found out is part of a whole other, very strange story, one that played out in front of forty million people, on the Russian answer to *Oprah*. But we'll get to that later.

That first summer a wonderful Russian doctor, Oleg Gordeyev, and a team of interpreters came to Ireland with the children and visited us regularly. I had an instant rapport with many of them – they loved our house because we were relaxed and easy-going. In fact, some of the main Russian players from the Chernobyl organisation joined To Russia With Love once I set it up, coming to work with us and giving me the immeasurable benefit of their wisdom and experience. One of them, Igor Stepanov, a translator, joined me almost on day one and has been my right hand ever since. He is a genius and a great friend, who has been indispensable. He is also the only man who can say no to me. My husband has never said no, in twenty-five years of marriage, and if he did, I can't imagine how I would take it. But Igor simply puts his foot down and I respect that, because he invariably knows what he's talking about. He understands Russia and Russian culture – the very real dangers and difficulties – in a way that I, even after fourteen years, don't.

Very quickly after Zina and Valya's arrival, I asked this support team whether it would be possible for us to adopt one of the girls. The team said yes, this was a possibility as both girls' names were formally registered for adoption. Another Irish family, by the way, later adopted Valya. She is still very close friends with Zina and is now the mother of a beautiful little girl, Emily. So I rang the host organisation and told them, 'Zina wants to stay and we want to keep her.'

Naturally, they thought I was being absurd and told me, 'Oh you'll settle down at the end of the month. You'll be delighted when it's time for them to go back!' They didn't like what we were doing at all; they thought it was a case of a 'puppy for Christmas' syndrome, that I was being far too emotional and would regret my decision. They had a point – very few people ever adopt children of that age and when they do, it is often a disaster. Zina was barely six months younger than Sophie – any decent adoption agency will insist couples only adopt a child much younger than the youngest of their other children, and rightly so. The pecking order is important within a family. Knowing as much as I do now about adoption – having seen so many go spectacularly wrong over the years – I shudder to think what might have been. But our gut instinct wasn't wrong. Our bond with Zina was as deep as it was instantaneous.

In response to the organisation's fears – they warned me, 'She'll be illegal in four weeks time. You can't keep her here' – I said, 'Let me sort that out.' Which was all very brave, but I was bluffing, I had absolutely no idea what to do. Then fate intervened. Zina started to get very bad headaches and not long afterwards she collapsed. We took her into Temple Street hospital, where they diagnosed meningitis. It was horrible. In order to find out which type she had, viral or bacterial, she had to have a lumbar puncture. Zina remained completely silent while the doctor put a huge needle into her spine and drained fluid. She put up with the pain in the same way she put up with everything else in life. A strange country, a strange hospital, a very large needle, an awful set of circumstances. If anything could have made our determination to keep her stronger, it was this.

Luckily, she had viral meningitis rather than bacterial. It's still serious, but far less likely to be fatal. However, on the up side, there was no way Zina could travel. Doctors at the hospital gave me letters to say that she couldn't fly for a year, so that bought us a bit of time and space to start proceedings. She wasn't legal, but neither was she going to be deported. This meant I could begin the absurd five-year process of trying to get the health board to approve Mick and I as adoptive parents, and that I could go to the Russian embassy and tell them what was going on, and ask for their help and support, which they most generously gave. In deciding to keep Zina with us, Mick and I embarked on a long, difficult and at times frustrating journey, one that changed our lives and the lives of our children completely, as well as the lives of many Russian children and Irish adults.

So why did we decide to keep Zina? Frankly, we hadn't thought it through, we simply didn't realise the enormity of what we were doing. That said, I always work with what my gut tells me – if something feels right, I do it. Zina herself said, from very early on, 'I'm not going back!' and we respected that. Also, I truly believed we could take on Zina's problems. A child who has had seven years in an institution is often a ticking time bomb in a normal family environment and I wasn't so naïve that I couldn't see that. Plus of course she was almost the same age as Sophie, another potential disaster, but I knew my family – Sophie has always been incredibly grounded and balanced, and I knew she would be able to deal with it. There is no doubt that over the years Zina has sucked up huge amounts of attention – back then, every time we went out, people would ask, 'So this is your little Russian one?' and coo over Zina, while Sophie would be standing there, so lovely, calm and wise, being totally overlooked. Even within the house, Zina was getting huge amounts of attention. We had Russian diplomats at the table, social workers knocking on the door, a camera crew under our feet, all for her. The entire conversation for years – nauseatingly, I'm sure – was Russia and Zina, and yet Sophie never had any problem with it at all. She was, and always has been, a wonderfully kind, wise and easy-going child. If she hadn't been, we couldn't have done it. As for Mikey, he was, from the second he was born, so adored and cosseted by me, Mick and Sophie, that nothing could have knocked him off his pedestal. And we did try hard to keep it balanced. Although a lot of attention inevitably went in Zina's direction, we made huge efforts not to make Sophie and Mikey feel less important. I think they would agree.

These days, Sophie, Zina and Mikey get on very well, unbelievably well I sometimes think. The success of the adoption lies in the dovetailing of their personalities. Sophie has always been the older sister, Mikey is still happy to be the baby and Zina was happy to slot into the middle. At times, like all siblings, they want to kill each other, but far less often than you'd expect.

We have an odd household, there's no doubt, but we're not combative at all; I might be noisy and bossy, but we don't fight. We are all very close, we eat together nearly every day – a combination of Apache Pizza, Chinese take-away and home cooking of course – and the children tell me an awful lot about their lives. Well, the girls do. Mikey tells us almost nothing.

Even as teenagers, none of them ever turned round and hurled bitter accusations, the way many teenagers might, about the time I spent away from them. The orphanage has also been a big part of their growing up and an incredible experience for them. They have made lasting friends there, even had love affairs. I am so lucky with my children.

During the first few years of the charity, every time I went away, I felt so guilty that I did the bribe thing. If I was going for five days, I would buy five presents for each of the three children and leave them with my mother to put under their pillows every morning. It might have been coloured pencils, or stickers, something tiny, anything to show them I was thinking about them. And I used to take my wedding and engagement rings off before each trip, in case I didn't make it back – then, at least, the girls would have a ring each. I gradually stopped doing that as I became more familiar with the comings and goings, even though the journeys can be dangerous. We have had narrow escapes and a couple of serious accidents along the way.

Two of the unsung heroes in all of this, people without whom I could never have done any of it, were my mother and my mother-in-law; both angels, one on each of my shoulders. My three were then the only grandchildren on both sides of the family and so I had these two remarkable women fighting over who got to mind our children and filling in for me whenever I wasn't there. Whenever I stepped out, my mother stepped in seamlessly. In fact, the children had three mothers really. Even now, although my mother-in-law very sadly died some years ago, my own mother still arrives at the house with the children's favourite dinners, cooked and ready to eat, several times a week. She brings grapes, curries, kedgeree and cookies, because she knows they love them, and it's her mission in life to spoil her grandchildren rotten. She has fresh flowers in my biggest vase after every trip, to this day. She has been an unflagging source of support all these years. In fact there is no describing my mammy. She is the most selfless person I know, without a doubt the best mother I have ever met. I am the envy of many because of Monny, as we call her.

Mick, too, made it easy for me – as easy as a man can when he sees such profound changes taking place in the woman he married. He is an amazing man, who has dedicated his entire life to being a father and is always there for the children. He has always been standing at the airport to meet me when I come home. He was instantly very close to Zina, closer probably than I would have been. He still goes out for walks with her every night and talks to her about anything that's on her mind, from idle chit-chat to more serious topics.

However, realistically, when you take on a project like To Russia With Love, at the level at which I took it on, you cannot be a full-time wife and mother too. Any energy I had left went to the children, so I suppose Mick got the worst end of the stick, in that often there was nothing left for him. I would be just too depleted and exhausted, or utterly distracted, to give him the attention he deserved. Yet he is an incredibly stoic person and put up with the fact that I was going off, for a week or ten days at a time, with other people, including other men, experiencing these incredibly intense events with them and bonding over shared moments, highs and lows, that he wasn't involved with. A lot of husbands wouldn't put up with that. I often thought Mick would have been better off if he had married someone else, had a different kind of wife, but I don't know if he would agree with that – I'm too afraid to ask! Certainly, there have been many very difficult moments. We're not a fighting pair, so there's no screaming, but we have had a few rough times along the way.

Financially I contributed nothing to the household for most of the years after To Russia With Love was established. Moreover, even when I was in Dublin, I was often out all day, and so doing no housework or cooking either, coming in totally stressed and going straight to bed. Mick meanwhile was keeping the whole show on the road financially, and would come home to find no dinner. Luckily he's very laid-back, so he would make his own dinner, with no complaint, and then – just like a man – walk away, leaving a pile of dishes in the sink. So one day I served up his dinner on the table, with no plate, just to prove a point. I cooked a particularly wet dinner and served it straight up. Mick just looked at me. He truly has huge reserves of patience and tolerance, and no ego. Quite a man. In fact, in all my forty-eight years, I have never met a better one.

Even so, I am amazed that we haven't divorced. I don't mean that in a funny way. We've even had conversations about which of the children and dogs would go where, only half joking. But we're still together, somehow. Marriage at its best is not easy, and my involvement with Russia made things that bit harder. He felt less important in my life because the project became everything. It's definitely been hard. But if I had married anyone else, it wouldn't have lasted, or I couldn't have done the work that I've done. No man I know would have been so kind, patient, selfless … the antithesis to me in fact.

In fairness, Zina herself was very easy. She tried incredibly hard to fit in from the very beginning. In fact, her biggest challenge really was that, like all orphan girls, she had learned very early to be an actress, to wear the colour of the season. Orphan girls play to please. They have to, to survive. This is why so many of them go on to please men, sadly, for money; it's one of the reasons prostitution is such a big problem once they leave the orphanages. Zina was cute enough to know that she needed to learn how to be a sister, a daughter, a granddaughter, very fast in order to manage the situation. She knew she had to be the perfect sibling to Mikey and Sophie, and so she was. She didn't try and displace anyone, because she could see immediately that it wasn't going to work, that it wouldn't be appreciated. And anyway, it's not in her nature. She's sweet and lovely and wants to help. Zina has always been very caring. All older children in orphanages raise the younger ones, because there aren't enough staff, so she would have been a big minder of Mikey from the start. At the time, we didn't realise how hard the poor little thing was working at trying to be all things to all of us. Looking back, I feel so sad for her, because I know now how hard she was trying and still tries.

For the first year, Zina regularly stored food under her bed. We didn't notice the food missing, but finally we realised she was hiding it because of the smell. Hoarding was simply second nature to her after seven years in an institution. Also, she found it terrifying to be in a room on her own – in the standard Russian orphanage there are thirty children to a room and they're used to that. So she wet the bed. Our house is a Victorian house, with a wobbly corridor upstairs and creaky floorboards. Zina was too scared to get up in the middle of the night and would never disturb us in case she'd get into trouble, so she bed-wet. It was very common with orphan children, often because in those days carers would give out to them if they got out of bed in the middle of the night.

Some would even humiliate them by hanging the soiled sheets out of their window to dry. Also the orphanage was freezing, the floors were always wet, there was never any toilet paper, rarely any bulbs and usually the toilets were blocked, so who would want to wee there? It meant the mattresses were often rancid, but the carers didn't mind – they didn't have to sleep on them. This is why so many Russian orphanages stank – it was the smell of stale urine. That was one of the first things we changed once we established To Russia With Love – we made beautiful toilets, pink and flowery, painted with roses, to try and encourage the children to use them. We also gave them furry slippers and teddy bears, to take the fear out of getting up at night. When we took over at Hortolova, 80 per cent of our children were bed-wetters. None of them are now.

Looking back, I'd say Zina was terrified deep down in those early days, but we never saw that. She was playing a role – the part of a bright, happy child – so desperate to fit in and stay that she couldn't let her guard drop for a moment. Children can do that. They compartmentalise. In order to survive, they have to be able to present a normal, happy face and box off all the hurt and pain.

Once Zina knew we were definitely keeping her, she did begin to make our house her own. She was no longer afraid of dark corners and could start to let her guard down. She realised she wasn't going to be reprimanded no matter what, because we're just not that sort of family, and this allowed her to finally relax.

2

I WILL COME BACK

For three years, we had Zina, but no papers; largely because the Eastern Health Board, as it was then, was a bit of a disaster and not very efficient. They made the whole process very difficult. At the start of it they told us we had to send Zina back to Russia, that it would take four to five years to complete our home assessment, and that only once it was finished could we go and collect her. She would have been twelve by then. I just couldn't believe it – so I challenged them. They wanted me to send a seven-year-old child back to an orphanage where she never had a visitor. I simply refused. I called their bluff. I said, 'I'm not sending her back. What are you going to do about it?' Which was all very well for me, but my mother lived in fear that she would be baby-sitting one day and someone would come up the garden path and simply take Zina back to Russia.

I was furious with the Eastern Health Board for being so unhelpful and so slow. And so I decided to see what the Russians could do for me. As it turned out, they were absolutely fantastic. I knocked on the door of the large, forbidding-looking embassy on Dublin's Orwell Road and said, 'I need to talk to you. I have a Russian child, I have no papers for her. Can you help me to keep her?' And they did.

The Russian embassy did a deal with me – as long as I agreed that they could call, unannounced, at any time, to our house, to Zina's school or to her doctor's, they would let her stay. That was fine with me. And they were as good as their word – they did call, frequently, sometimes with less than an hour's warning and often at dinnertime! We had to dash off to buy a tablecloth and a set of matching cutlery, because we had neither, and we had to work damn hard to impress. Russian mothers are very domesticated. They run orderly houses, they bake and they sew, so we needed to look as if we did all of those things. I cook, but I don't bake, so my mother would be on stand-by, ready to whip an apple tart out of the oven.

I was completely unfamiliar with having diplomats in the house and Russian diplomats in particular are very formal, so I had to learn all manner of things, like how to address them, who to speak to first, what order to serve food in. Zina meanwhile would hide upstairs and refuse point-blank to speak Russian to them, because her fear was always – and still is – that they would take her back. We got ourselves into some hilarious situations, trying to appear as the perfect family for Zina's sake – like the day I got an hour's notice that the consul and his wife were coming to tea. I rang Mick and asked him to go to a deli on Francis Street where you could buy these pastry plaits, with chicken or salmon in them, that were half-cooked – you bunged them in the oven for fifteen minutes and they came out looking delicious and just as if you had made them yourself. So Mick arrived back with one of the plaits, I popped it in the oven and discreetly hid the box in the bins out the back. The consul and his wife duly arrived, and I produced this plait, looking golden brown and smelling wonderful. The consul's wife, a terribly formal, though nice, lady said, 'What's in the pie? I am allergic to fish.' Well, I had no idea whether Mick had bought a chicken or salmon plait. I don't think even he knew. So there I was, trying to stall for time by blathering on about how it was an old family recipe, while I cut into the pie, desperately trying to see which one it was! Luckily it was chicken. On the same visit, Mikey, then a fat little three-year-old, pushed a kids' wheelbarrow through our glass kitchen door, which shattered. The door itself landed right beside where we were dining. Later, he donned his superman suit and jumped off the landing into the hall as they left. I tried to bundle the Russians out the door before the screaming started.

We had lots of funny, tense moments like that, but in the end we became extremely friendly with the Russian embassy staff. We had parties for them, dinners, Christmas drinks. We did it for Zina, to persuade them that we were the right people to care for her, but we began to enjoy it too. And for many of those Russians, this was the first time they had ever been inside an Irish home. It was a learning curve for all of us. The Russians could not have been nicer.

At the same time as Mick and I were wooing the Russian embassy, we were also submitting to the absurdities of the Eastern Health Board adoption assessment. I'm perfectly certain now that, had we not already had Zina, there is no way we would ever have qualified to adopt – despite being loving parents to our own two children. There was so much box-ticking to be done and they asked the most shocking and sometimes outrageous questions. I simply refused to answer, because I couldn't see how they had any bearing on the case.

For example, 'Have you ever had a miscarriage?' As a matter of fact I had, two, as it happens, but they weren't huge dramas in my life. They happened, I cried and it was awful, but I got over it, moved on and had my adored Mikey. They were very much in my past. But the health board wanted to know, 'When was the first time you had sex with your husband after the miscarriage?' Now, although this is a deeply intrusive question, I can see it might have some relevance to a couple with no children looking to adopt – no sex life might be an indicator of trouble in the marriage for example – but it had absolutely nothing to do with our situation. And so I said, 'I'm not answering that, you are simply being nosey.'

To be honest, over a cup of coffee, I would quite likely have told their representative the answer, but it was the irrelevance that annoyed me. Mick, who is a real pacifist, would say, 'Just answer the question, and let's just get through this.' But I couldn't.

Most couples who find themselves in that situation are desperate to have children and so when the social worker comes in, in order to pass the test, they put up with what I think are inappropriate questions so that they look like the perfect parents. In my case, our adopted child was right there, I had the support of the Russian government and I was sending her nowhere, so I thought, 'To hell with you if you think I'm going to help tick your little boxes.' Any questions that I considered relevant, I answered, but no others.

I have always believed that the Irish government is against foreign adoption. I still watch couples fight unreasonable obstacles to get their babies; young social workers assessing adults in their mid-thirties or mid-forties, who have been through the mill, and making life-changing judgements about them. It's not right. I do understand there have to be rules to avoid appalling things like people going into foreign countries and stealing babies, and of course to avoid paedophiles taking children from institutions. However, there also has to be some scope for an individual approach, an assessment based on the specific case. I feel we were one of these, but the Eastern

Health Board couldn't cope with 'individual'. There were boxes to be ticked and we didn't fit them.

I hoped the system would have changed by now, but it seems not. A friend attended an Irish Adoption Authority meeting recently and described the scene: one hundred and fifty Irish couples in the room, most of them five years in the queue to adopt. Some left in tears, some walked out. These couples are trying to give a child a home, not commit a crime, although they felt no one would necessarily have known that. Thankfully, the current chair of the Adoption Authority, Geoffrey Shannon, has a heart and a brain and a willingness to look at the situation. It appears that Frances Fitzgerald, Minister for Children, is supporting him. Let's see if they can bring about the change that their predecessors never managed. I'm not sure how much hope I hold out, but they may prove me wrong.

The intrusive questions weren't the only part of the process that annoyed me. We were being assessed with a group of other prospective adoptive parents – none of whom had children. And so this group was being taught the ABC of child-rearing, including how to bath a baby, using a doll. Mick and I had two children, one of whom, Mikey, was only three, and we wanted to adopt a seven-year-old. We really didn't need to learn how to bath babies, but would they let us skip any of it, no matter how basic? No. They had boxes to be ticked. If we didn't learn how to bath that doll, they couldn't proceed. I was totally frustrated by them. I may have been being overly sensitive, but I hated them coming to our house, asking, 'How do you discipline your children?' The fact was we didn't discipline them, we are a very laid-back household and saw no need for the 'naughty step', 'time out' or any of the things they were advocating. I found it all incredibly irritating and they seemed to have no understanding of our attitude. It was a difficult situation.

Just to add a little extra pressure to what was already an incredibly hectic time – we also had a camera crew in the house during all of this. TV3 were filming us for a documentary – it would be shown in 1999 as *To Russia With Love*. The cameras were there nearly 24/7 – because of course what they really want is to catch you having a meltdown at midnight. So there they were, filming everything as we entertained the Russians, suffered the health board inefficiency and tried to help Zina to learn some of the things that would have been second nature to any Irish seven-year-old, such as how to choose clothes in the morning. Having come from an orphanage where she had only one set of clothes, it was terrifying for her to be sent upstairs and told to get dressed, because she would have to choose between seven pairs of tights and a cupboard full of dresses. We'd go up after half an hour and find her standing there, panicked, unable to make up her mind. Choice is a luxury that orphans don't understand.

By this time, several months into her life with us, Zina was starting to speak English and we were finally able to communicate with her, beyond the basic language of hugs and physical affection. She began to talk to us about the children she had left behind, her classmates from the orphanage. She was lamenting not seeing them, in particular Valya, who was back in Russia before her formal adoption by another Irish family, and one boy called Pasha, whose photo she kept beside her bed. I didn't fully understand it at the time, but these children were as close as siblings. They had grown up together and looked to one another for solace and support. They shared every waking moment. In the absence of enough adults to care for them, love them and protect them, they had, in some cases, forged these bonds of affection among themselves. Zina came originally from a place called Klintsy, a small, well-run baby orphanage. However, in general orphanages were a bit like a scene from *Lord of the Flies* – the children existed in their own world, in which their relationships with each other took the place of family.

Much of that only became clear to me later, but I did understand that Zina had a seven-year history with these children and that I had simply lifted her out of that life and plonked her into our nice home in Clontarf, with a ready-made set of grandparents, uncles, aunts and cousins. I could see that I had left behind her entire world – exactly as some

American evangelists who come to Russia these days to adopt deliberately tend to do. The difference is that I felt this was wrong, that there had to be some continuity to Zina's life, so I promised her that I would go to Russia, find her classmates in the orphanage, tell them that she was okay and try to establish some type of communication.

I still can't believe how naïve and ignorant I was. How totally unprepared I was for what had been the realities of Zina's life before we took her in. But even if I had known then what I know now, I would have made that first trip.

It was very difficult even to find the orphanage where her class had been moved to after she left Russia. Russian orphanages tend to be buried in the middle of deep woods, far from any towns or cities, and Hortolova was no different. A friend, Caroline Mahon, came with me and we flew to Minsk from Shannon, then travelled another nine hours by car through Belarus before getting to the Russian border. Eventually, after a night's sleep and another two hours' driving, we walked through the gates of this overgrown, dilapidated, forgotten place, like a derelict factory, where the grass grew higher than the windows. It was like walking into a different world, or even a different century, somewhere wild and forgotten. It was September, a beautiful month in Russia, but very cold, and nothing worked in the orphanage. Igor and Dr Oleg, who I met through the organisation that first brought

Zina to Ireland, used their connections to organise our access, so we could wander at will. The heating was broken and the freezing wind whistled through the broken windowpanes. The children were wearing cheap, plastic shoes that had holes in them and certainly didn't keep the cold out. Many of them had no jackets. The kitchens were filthy, with the kind of deep, ingrained dirt that seemed to have been laid down over years, and there wasn't a single working toilet for 200 children.

The boys' block smelled like the lion's enclosure at the zoo – that over-powering urine smell – and the boys were simply shitting on the ground of the bathrooms. The girls were cleaner about themselves, although their toilets weren't working either. I just couldn't believe the conditions these children were living in. The dormitories were huge, filled with jangly old steel beds, like a military hospital, with great piles of dirty clothes everywhere, and dogs sleeping on them. There were piles of filthy clothes up to the ceiling in the laundry room. The smell everywhere was disgusting. The children themselves were filthy. What was hardest for me in a way was their teeth – none of them had ever seen a toothbrush, let alone a dentist, and all their teeth were covered in a kind of greenish gunk. Oh, and they all had rats. As pets. Fully grown white rats with long pink tails. They kept them in their beds, carried them around in their jumpers.

It was a terrible place. One little girl, a tiny little slip of a thing, had the shape of an iron burned onto her face, as though she had been branded. Sadly, bullying is endemic in these institutions and wherever there are humans there will be abusers, so we were on guard.

Worse even than the physical hardship was the fact that no one seemed to be minding these children. There was no sign of anyone in charge, although many random people were wandering around and appeared to have no role. It all felt incredibly unprotected. I was bowled over by the danger of it and stunned that we were just three hours by plane from London. There I was, wrapped up in my lovely warm jacket and I was bringing sweets to these children who didn't even have the basic necessities of life. I thought, 'How ridiculous, how stupid we are that we would even come to a place like this with sweets.'

In one of the huge dormitories, a girl was lying in her bed, sobbing. She was bruised all over, black and blue. Through Lena, our interpreter, I asked, 'What's wrong with you?' She told us that one of the boys had beaten her, so I went and found the boy and read him the riot act. I told him never to raise a hand to a girl again, how dared he, and so on. I must have thought I was going to solve all the problems of the world in one week. It was ridiculous. But to Sasha, the girl who had been beaten, I was her saviour. She held my hand for the entire week I was there and when it came time for us to

47

leave, she didn't want to let me go. I had my arms around her, saying goodbye, and she said to our interpreter, 'Tell Debbie I've never been kissed before.' She was nine years old.

Until then, I hadn't intended to come back. I had found Zina's classmates, had given them all sweets and a letter from her, and made some vague promises. I intended to pack a bag of toys, and maybe some old clothes, and send them out. But Sasha wasn't letting me go. I was crying, she was crying. And that comment of hers just broke me. It hit me like a ton of bricks, along with the misery and neglect all around us. It also made me realise that I could do something. I thought, 'Well, I can't fix the place and I can't rebuild this old building, but I can come back and hug this child.' And so I made her a promise. 'I will come back, and I will kiss you and hug you on your birthday.'

Since that moment, I have always had a special relationship with Sasha, but I couldn't be seen to be doting specifically on her, it wouldn't have been fair, and so my mother sponsored her as part of the programme we set up to connect loving Irish families with our Russian children. The two of them became best buddies and have written to one another for years. My mum is like her mother; they have a very close relationship. For my mother's seventieth birthday a couple of years ago, we flew Sasha in at our own expense, secretly, and she carried in the cake. It was a very special moment. These days, Sasha is training to be a hairdresser and waitressing in the meantime. She's such a bright girl, but because To Russia With Love wasn't created in time to intervene with her earliest schooling, she didn't go on to university. Hairdressing is a good career, but because she's an orphan she's never going to work in a top salon. All it takes is one question – who's your father? – and these children are stigmatised. Most Russians only have one child and pour all their resources into them. The gap between 'family children', as we call them, and our orphanage children is just huge.

As I said goodbye to Sasha and the other children on that cold September day, they all crowded around us, begging us to stay and even barred the gates to stop us leaving. I had no idea that this second promise of mine – to come back – would mean that fourteen years later I would still be trying to keep faith with the children of Russia's orphanages.

3

I DON'T WORK
WITH DUMB BLONDES

I had made my promise to Sasha and I sobbed all the way home. I had a complete meltdown. Suddenly Zina seemed to have so much, because these children had literally nothing. They were living in squalor, with just enough to eat, no treats, no playgrounds, no toys, nothing to cheer or brighten their days. It was unbearable. Times were brutally hard in 1998 all over Russia, as their economy had just crashed.

Once home, I think I sat at the kitchen table in a daze for about a week, crying most of the time. I am lucky to be surrounded by amazing friends in Clontarf and, one by one, they all began sitting round the kitchen table too. The key has been in our door for twenty years, we've never taken it out. People just let themselves in and out of our house all the time, although they do have to run the gauntlet of our 75 kilogram Leonberger dog, who looks like a not-terribly-small lion. The story was coming out bit by bit, and I had photographs. Soon

I had them all crying. I knew I had to do something.

I decided to have a coffee morning, supported by some great women and cake bakers, like a typical Irish housewife! My timing was perfect. My neighbours in Clontarf were all young mums, their husbands were doing well and they were all looking for a story. I gave them one. Also, we had just renovated our house, a Victorian house (which hasn't been renovated since I might add) and people were dying to have a look around. So we advertised this coffee morning and there was a queue to get into my house until midnight that night. Around midday we decided to add whiskey, switch to Irish coffee and charge more. We raised about £7,000, which was huge money. The *Sunday Independent* gave us a bit of coverage and suddenly the whole thing began gathering momentum. My landline at home never stopped ringing – people pledging old clothes, toys, offering to have their own coffee mornings; the minute I put the phone down, it would ring again.

My big decision then was what to spend the money on, this £7,000 we'd raised from the coffee morning. We equipped a convoy – trucks carrying the donated clothes, toys, food, blankets and so on. Incidentally, it's one of only two we ever did. These days, I just don't do convoys. In my experience, either you get black bags full of dirty clothes and jigsaws with pieces missing or, if it's any good, the stuff arrives in the front door of the institution and goes straight out the back door. There are exceptions, obviously; Liam Grant's charity in Waterford does it well, and I'm sure there are others, but it's not for me.

I decided to spend the rest of the money, not on Christmas presents for the children, which was my first idea, but on bringing out a doctor, a nurse – an extraordinary woman called Trish McGrath, who became one of the key founders of To Russia With Love – a builder, journalist Mary O'Sullivan and photographer Dave Conachy, both from the *Sunday Independent*. The plan was for the trip to be a fact-finding mission – how much needed to be done, realistically – and to try and get a story into the paper to help us raise more money to do it.

So this fact-finding team went out, in November 1998, in minus 30ºC. We all met in the airport for the first time. One of the team was John Mulligan, a founder of Trade Aid, an author and human rights worker, who is still a close friend, but initially was absolutely scathing about how I was operating. John is a very serious person, a brilliant humanitarian, and one of my mentors, but we couldn't stand each other in the beginning. He couldn't bear how shallow I was. He was right. Or at least a little bit right.

Mulligan is an extraordinary individual, a fighter for great causes who takes bullshit from no one and fights battles others are afraid of. He carries a month of ironed shirts in his tiny carry-on bag, as well as alarm systems, wires and tools – it's like Mary Poppins' bag! He never drinks, is always lethally astute, terrifying at times and a big cuddly bear in his Russian raccoon fur hat. I love him dearly and am honoured to be a friend and ally to this day.

He thought I was another Anneka Rice and happily informed me I was a classic dumb blonde who planned to fly in, paint everything pink, fly out and have everyone feel great about themselves. And he was probably right in a way – I did think it could be a quick fix, a six-month job, then back to my life. I was initially naïve about the can of worms I was opening. Anyway, we had a stand-up row, but somehow made up and he agreed to come with us. Once there, he got completely and utterly immersed in what we were doing and came back many times. On one memorable trip that I can recall, we were at Gatwick airport, the computer systems were down, everything was total chaos and there wasn't even coffee to be had. A very hungry John Mulligan proceeded to tell the girl on the desk, very seriously, that the two Russians with us would defect if we weren't put through to the VIP area immediately. Goal achieved! We were swept through and a big breakfast was ordered airside.

We did a big week at the orphanage, a full assessment of what the place needed. At the same time, even though we didn't yet have funds, I began talking to the Department of Education in Bryansk, who had responsibility for all the orphanages in the area, about the possibility of coming back and renovating block by block. Their attitude was that if we wanted to come back with building and childcare experts, they would happily work with us. This was the beginning of a beautiful friendship.

Mark Wheeler, our doctor, examined the children and diagnosed something called psycho-social deprivation – through lack of love, they weren't growing. They were much smaller than the national average. A recent report indicated that even now, although conditions are much improved, every five months children in Russian orphanages fall one month behind in average weight and growth. Back then, Dr Wheeler likened it to a plant without enough water; they were getting basic food requirements but only the bare minimum, and no love, so they simply couldn't thrive normally. They also had head lice and scabies, many of them were raw from it. Once scabies gets into an orphanage, it's really hard to stop, it goes through the place like wildfire. We looked for signs of abuse among the children, not obsessively, but we did look, we had to. And luckily, we found no evidence that this was happening. The problems were neglect, lack of love, lack of attention and of course the grinding poverty that is part of rural life for the majority of Russians who live in small towns. It wasn't just these orphan children who were living in squalor and deprivation – the local villages were almost as bad, although we didn't see or notice that at first, because we were so overwhelmed by what needed to be done for the children.

We're not supposed to have favourite children, but, somehow, if you happen to be there the day a child arrives, there will always be something particularly close in that bond. I remember the day two little girls, Lena and Raya, aged nine and six, arrived in. They were from a quite well-heeled family – their father owned a restaurant – and should never have been there, but their father had murdered their mother. The families didn't want these two little girls, so they were put into care. They arrived in nice clothes and clearly weren't the average orphan child, so some of the staff resented them and were sometimes cruel. It always reminded me of that Frances Hodgson Burnett story, *A Little Princess*, where she has to live in the attic after her father dies and there's no money left.

Lena and I always had a very strong bond. She saved all her grieving for the times I was there, we would sit on her bed for hours, dealing with the tears. Two years ago when she got married she invited me to the wedding. Her father spent fifteen years in prison and was released about eighteen months ago, and Lena had to take him in. He had nowhere to go. There are no hostels, no halfway houses in Russia, nobody wants him and there's no social welfare system to look after him. So now Lena lives with her new husband and the man who killed her mother. She has a huge set of problems dealing with that, because she loved her mother. And yet he's her father. If she didn't take him in, he had nowhere else to go.

Another girl, Catya, a stunningly beautiful child, was given up to us about five years ago, when she was twelve. Her mother found a new man and simply said, 'I'm moving on with my life, you can have her.' Catya hasn't seen her since. She's seventeen now, still absolutely beautiful and one of our brightest children. She's currently on the scholarship programme sponsored by Kellogg's and gets everything she needs. But her mother has never been back, not once. It never ceases to amaze me. What mothers in the world choose to give up their babies? Yet sometimes in Russia they seem to do it without a backward glance.

Despite all the trauma, tears are not common in orphanages. They are a sign of weakness and, anyway, no one responds, so the children don't bother crying. If you go into a baby orphanage, they are silent places. It's the saddest sound on earth. When we came to Hortolova first, there was silence. As the Irish got under their skin, the children became noisier and bolder. They gained the confidence to express themselves.

That second, fact-finding trip was an incredible experience for the team who travelled. There was a lot of hysterical laughing, a lot of hysterical tears. We were all on a monstrous learning curve. My head was spinning with what I needed to do. My plan was to try to renovate the orphanage – these days, you probably wouldn't do that, because the thinking now is, that the longer we keep renovating them, the longer they'll be there, and that residential care, which means small houses with a maximum of ten children, mimicking family life, is a better option. But in 1998 I had no better solution. It was minus 30°C and there was no glass in most of the windows, or any central heating. We needed to get the children through the winter and there just wasn't a different plan. 'Let's not dream about changing society, let's get glass in the windows' was our thinking.

Back home I thought, 'What on earth do I do now?' I had no money – we'd used it on the trip – so I thought, 'To hell with it, I'll ring Pat Kenny and see if he'll put me on *Kenny Live*.' So I rang RTÉ and they said, 'Who are you?' and I said, 'I'm really nobody. I'm a housewife from Clontarf, I need to ask Pat Kenny if he'll put me on, because I need to talk to Ireland.' To his great credit, Pat Kenny came on the phone. These days you undoubtedly wouldn't get him, but I was lucky. I asked him, 'Would you mind putting me on the show on Saturday night for ten minutes? I want to tell a story about an orphanage in Russia which badly needs Irish help.' He said, 'Can you talk?' I said I could, and he said, 'Come on so.' We were then in the process of formally registering To Russia With Love as an Irish charity and opened an Irish bank account in time for the TV appearance.

It was a very emotive show. Zina was sitting in the front row, looking sweet and gorgeous, along with my husband, the rest of my family, Trish McGrath, my right arm for many years, and the team that had travelled. I explained what we were doing and why. And for anyone who missed *Kenny Live* on the Saturday night, the *Sunday Independent* had a double page spread the next morning, with Mary O'Sullivan's first article and Dave Conachy's fabulous photos of the children. It was a double whammy and it began to yield results almost immediately.

On the Monday morning, a man with an American accent rang me, saying, 'I'm just going to lodge $25,000.' I thought it was my husband messing – Mick would do something stupid like that – so I asked him, 'What time are you home for your dinner?' Then I put the phone down and thought, 'Maybe it wasn't Mick messing.' The very next day, $25,000 dollars arrived from the Bahamas. This man had been in Ireland, at a funeral, and had bought the *Sunday Independent*. He went straight home and lodged money to our account. I was beginning to understand the power of the media.

That was the beginning of a remarkable snowball. The TV3 documentary about our adoption of Zina came out at about the same time and things really took off. The Celtic Tiger had just been born and there were men's lunches, ladies' lunches, auctions and charity balls galore. We were in the right place at the right time, and we had the weight of the *Sunday Independent* behind us, which was amazing, because I wasn't a socialite, I wasn't glamorous, we were just very ordinary Irish people, whose lives were about to change completely.

Following the *Kenny Live* appearance and the *Sunday Independent* article, the money started to pour in and we were swamped with goodwill. At that stage, the 'office', such as it was, was still in my house, and the phone was going mental, from morning 'til night. I think people were so moved, even inspired, by the idea of tackling something achievable. We weren't trying to feed Africa, or cure AIDS, we were trying for something tangible and definable – to rebuild an orphanage with 200 children in it and give them better lives. Incredible people came on board from an early stage, offering to help, asking to go out to Russia with us.

We formed a board very quickly, made up entirely of parents from my local area. Our accountant, Fergal McGrath, was telling me to be strategic, to find a shrewd businessman, a consultant, a solicitor, all of whom would have provided different fields of expertise, but I didn't. My gut feeling was to ask friends of mine, school-gate moms and dads, just like me, who were driven to do this by the desire to help children. All of those people are still patrons of the charity and are still very close friends.

My house was completely consumed by To Russia With

Love, and our health board home assessment was going on also. I was on the phone endlessly, talking to volunteers and fund-raisers, and sorting out problems. Not everybody was genuinely trying to help; I got a call one morning, the week after *Kenny Live*, to say there was a man out in Tallaght selling paintings door-to-door that our children had apparently done in the orphanage! Obviously he was a total fake, profiting from the publicity we had received, but it had never occurred to me that someone would do such a thing, so I was completely thrown by it at first.

One day I was on the phone, yet again, when Zina, who by then was able to speak and write a smattering of English, held up a sign in front of me, trying to get my attention – 'I don't feel well, can I have Calpol?' The social workers would have loved that! I finally realised that we would have to move out. We got a tiny office down the road, which a travel agent in Clontarf kindly gave to us for free, and we took the decision to employ someone full-time. Up until then, we were all just volunteers, although many of us were working flat out.

Our wonderful accountant advised us very clearly and cleverly from the start. He was ruthlessly transparent and strict with us. We weren't allowed to open post, and aren't to this day, without two members of staff being there. This is simply one of the many governance rules he implemented. Certainly, I've never been allowed sole access to any charity money in fourteen years. Thanks to Fergal, from the very beginning we have had a clear paper trail of every single donation, every penny given, in all our years. We have been unbelievably, painfully transparent, which has been hard. I am very undisciplined personally with my own money, so at times the constraints of our transparency drive me nuts. And then people complain that charities have admin costs, but if you have good governance, you have to have admin costs, it's as simple as that! Nevertheless, we have always been incredibly vigilant about where people's money goes. Any salary ever paid by us has been minimal. Thankfully, the staff we have do this as a labour of love. We pay them just enough to make that possible.

None of the board was taking a salary or expenses. For the first twelve years, I was the same – paid nothing. My husband supported me completely, even though he ran his own small business and we were never wealthy; in fact, the household could really have done with a second salary. Nevertheless, he supported me financially without complaint, as he so generously does in everything I do. However, about two years ago, at the recommendation of an external auditor, I agreed to accept €25,000 a year. The auditor felt that my financial dependence on my husband was a weakness of the charity, and that if anything happened to his earning power, both the charity and I would be badly affected. I agreed, under considerable pressure from my board, all of whom are serious financial people who watch our admin costs like a bunch of hawks to make sure the maximum possible amount of money goes where it is needed most – to the children. The salary does not sit well with me – even though it is a fraction of that paid to senior personnel by so many other charities, and although I work a sixty-hour week and never turn my phone off. That is something that I do quite naturally and was certainly doing for all the years before any salary was part of the equation. These days I find it simply unsustainable given the reduced level of donations and so, after two-and-a-half years of receiving it, have decided to cease taking it, whatever the auditor might say.

Even so, I have been accused of stealing from the charity. One guy in a restaurant, after the TV3 documentary came out, suggested that my new kitchen, visible in the documentary, had been paid for out of charity money. I wanted to punch him. I certainly stormed out. I was working so hard at that stage, we were all killing ourselves morning, noon and night, and the idea that anyone could think we were stealing from the children just shocked me! In fairness, I got flowers and an apology to the office the next day, he said he'd thought about what he'd said and regretted it. However, it did make me very aware of the kinds of things the cynical and suspicious could think, which in turn made me all the more determined to keep admin costs down and be able to account for every penny donated.

On one of the early visits, a volunteer who worked as a childcare expert for the health board came out with us. He spent time in the orphanage and wrote a report back to the To Russia With Love board. His advice was to walk away, on the basis that we couldn't make a difference to children when there were so few of us on the ground. He insisted that we needed one-to-one care, night care and day care; that we would be taking all this money out of Ireland and that even so we couldn't make a difference, because we didn't have enough people to change the system. I badly needed him to endorse what I was doing, so when I read this report, I thought, 'Bloody hell! I hope he's wrong, because we're not going to give it up!' I gave it to the board, but we decided to battle on and just wrap our arms around as many children as we could, to try and help them. It's been a fight from day one. Every single thing we've managed to achieve has been a tremendous battle.

Initially, we were on a mission to rebuild the orphanage, but very quickly I became caught up in rebuilding the children.

4

THE WIZARD OF OZ

Someone said to me recently, 'There must be times when you feel out of your depth.' I thought about it and realised that, no, there aren't. I hate sounding arrogant, but, I'm forty-eight years of age and I actually feel I could walk into a room with the president of America at this stage and not be intimidated. He might know things I don't, but I'm sure I know more about some things than he does.

I think I must always have felt like this. I'm not easily impressed, and certainly not by smoke and mirrors. That stood to me when I came face to face with my Russian colleagues. In Russia, you can't move unless you go to the top, so that's what I did. There was no point giving out to the staff in the orphanages, who were nearly as miserable as the children. They were only doing what they were told, following the regulations that had been laid down for the care of orphan children decades ago and never changed. They may have been initially without imagination or much affection in their handling of the children, but there was little else they could do under the circumstances. To effect change, I needed to go above their heads, to where the real power was.

My first meeting with a governor of Bryansk was exactly like the scene in *The Wizard of Oz* where Dorothy gets an audience with the wizard. The doors into the wizard's office are 100 feet high, down corridors that are kilometres long, and it's exactly the same in Russia; the further you walk, the smaller you feel. It's part of a whole pompous show, designed to make you believe the wizard is real and to intimidate anyone at a lower level. I've never seen bigger tables than those in Russian offices, so big you can fit thirty-five armchairs around them. There were usually soldiers with guns standing out the front and legions of minions all bowing and scraping to the governor. All my Russian interpreters were terrified by the sheer scale of things, but for me, it was just the same as having some little man hiding behind the curtains, working the levers. I loved the drama of it.

I found that once I got face-to-face with the governor, despite the Charvet shirts, secretaries and assistants, I could see he was only human. When I told him his orphanages were a bloody disgrace, my interpreters were all horrified, but he actually responded like a human being. In fact, I was nearly always able to establish a good rapport with these men – yes, they were always men! – and appeal to their basic decency, as well as all the other things us girls can appeal to. My interpreters wondered how I succeeded in getting them on side, but I think it was precisely because I didn't treat them like the Wizard of Oz. I treated them as human beings and they responded as such. Plus, a bottle of Jameson often helped!

However, that said, the good sense of my interpreters and guides did protect me from a lot of ignorant blunders. At some of my first meetings, when I would be ranting about the awful conditions in the orphanages, these interpreters made the unilateral decision simply not to translate for me! Recently, I looked back at one of the TV3 documentaries, made in the very early days, at a scene in which I'm saying to a high-up Russian official, 'I cannot *believe* the state the orphanages are in, this is disgusting and inhumane ...!' Now that I speak a bit of Russian, I can see that Igor, my wonderful interpreter, is conveying this, cautiously, and hilariously I now think, as, 'Debbie feels the conditions could be better ...' I'd say Igor's caution is one of the reasons I'm still working in Russia. He was cleverly diffusing the whole conversation because he knew that you absolutely don't hurl insults at a governor. I was just indignant that they were treating children so badly and I didn't know any better. Also, by then we had money, Irish money, donated by kind-hearted people and the Department of Foreign Affairs in Ireland, and so we went to the highest level of government in our region to ensure we sent this money exactly where it was most needed.

I mean, what on earth do you do with an orphanage in another country that's falling down? I hadn't a clue. I didn't know where to start. Do you knock it down? Fix it up? Ideally we should have been knocking it down and starting residential care, but it was too soon in Russia to do that. These days, that would be the way to go, but fourteen years ago, Russia simply wasn't ready. There was no possibility of finding homes for these orphans, so instead we asked the children what they wanted us to do, beginning with the girls' block. They asked for a haven of pink, the same as a Barbie castle we had bought them, so that's what we decided to do, build them a Barbie house.

At the time there were about 200 children in Hortolova, ranging in age from six to eighteen years, everything from sweet little six-year-old girls, up to eighteen-year-old boys who were so fierce they looked like they might knife you. These boys had been institutionalised all their lives and some were very aggressive. Also, what I didn't realise at the time was that Hortolova had been formed only a year earlier, essentially from the unwanted of other orphanages. The most difficult, demanding children, or those with the most complicated paperwork, from all over the region, had been taken out of other orphanages and put together in this terrible place. The authorities did a clean-out, because these other orphanages were getting too big – there were around 4,000 orphans in the region at that stage – and so they opened up this ancient, dilapidated building and filled it with children who were aggressive, withdrawn or had never attended school. The children who needed extra care and attention, essentially, were just dumped here and forgotten about.

The big boys were hard to love – initially – because they trusted no one. However, over time we built huge relationships with many of them. The little ones, they broke all our hearts immediately. They were holding our hands, giving us whatever little scrap of things they had – teddy bears, food they saved from their dinner plates – begging us to stay. You end up thinking, how can I leave this child behind? And in such dire conditions? Hortolova in those days was a disgusting place for children and those children were sad, uncared for and unloved. They were fed, that was about it. State staff, then, were suspicious of foreigners, poor, overworked, under-motivated and treated appallingly by their superiors.

It made me furious. And very determined. I've come to respect the Russians more over the years, because I understand more now. I know their budgets are bad and I also know now what I didn't then – standards in villages in Russia, where all of these orphanages are located, are generally terrible. Initially, we only saw the orphanages and didn't realise that many of the villagers were living in similar conditions. Frankly, in comparison with the general standard, the orphanages weren't even that bad. In a way, the hardship faced by everyone in rural Russia means that when our children do leave, often they can settle down in the local village, get married and no one much minds. Although orphans are very definitely stigmatised, everyone is so unbelievably suspicious and untrusting that they hardly notice who lives next door. These traits are born out of a very difficult history that Russian people have suffered for so long.

The general, grinding poverty meant that theft was a huge problem in the early days. For example, in Russia there were no mops. None at all. The accepted method of cleaning a floor was a dirty old cardigan on the end of a toothless sweeping brush. To this day, Trisha and I regret we didn't open a mop company – we would be multimillionaires. We brought mops with us on every single trip and they were so big a part of our operation that one of our regular workers used to introduce them to people on the plane: 'Mop, meet Michael. Michael, meet Mop ...' The women in the orphanages were delighted, they would be admiring these mops, saying, 'My God, it's fantastic ...' And by the time we came back again, every single one would have disappeared. I'll never forget the speed with which our fabulous mops and buckets vanished!

For the second, and last, convoy we ever did, we had these big, fancy hospital buckets, costing €300–€400 a pop, that had been donated. I was becoming obsessed with cleaning products – if I visited someone in Beaumont Hospital, I would be taking pictures of the industrial buckets; and as for McDonald's, forget the vanilla shakes, have you seen their mops? They departed in a truck along with all the other stuff, but a week later, when we arrived by plane to begin training, there wasn't a single one left! We gave up doing convoys, realising that it was a much better idea to bring in money and spend it in Russia. By contributing to the local economy and buying Russian items for the children, we reduced the amount of resentment felt by the villagers and made it less likely that the stuff would be stolen. Theft was perfectly understandable in the circumstances and once we copped on to this the renovation ran much more smoothly.

In fact, the only reason we did that particular convoy, was because of a horse called 'Debbie's Dream', made by a young man serving a long stretch in Wheatfield Prison. I knocked on the prison door at a very early stage of To Russia With Love, because someone had told me that prisoners could make playgrounds. It was part of their rehabilitation – they designed and manufactured playgrounds for residential care units in Ireland and I wanted one for Russia. The assistant governor, an amazing man called Derek Tracy, allowed me into his office – and I'd say he regrets it to this very day! He became my mentor, travelling companion, psychiatrist and friend. He was a true blue civil servant, someone who understood the system and how to make it work. He taught me how to do what I needed to do, how to make things happen in Russia. He has spent ten years travelling with To Russia With Love and was a major cog in the wheel. Without him, there is no way I could have done what I did. He put fun into everything and on our grimmest of days he had us all hysterically laughing at something random ... and Russia certainly does random!

For example, in Russia, orphanage regulations were laid out many decades ago, and are rigid and almost unchangeable. This kind of thing was incredibly frustrating for me, because I wanted to change everything now, now, now! Clean kitchens, working toilets, toys, good food, warm shoes ... and wheels just don't turn like that in Russia, they grind slowly. Derek Tracy trained us all in what is needed to get an institution from the lowest level up to something acceptable. There is a huge similarity between orphanages and prisons – from day one you should be training them to leave – except that, as Derek pointed out, our children have committed no crime.

Derek worked brilliantly with the Russian administration. He had respect for each and every one of the staff members, and fully understood their frustrations and boundaries. I, however, did not.

My very small payback to Derek was that I agreed to meet the prisoners and give talks, telling them about the children. They love people coming in, because it brightens up the prison day. So I went in quite a lot. One day one of the prisoners told me he had a surprise for me in the workshop – it was a stunningly carved, hand-painted rocking horse, the size of a donkey, with a leather saddle and a brass plaque on the foot of it saying 'Debbie's Dream'. The prisoner, deeply suspicious, asked me to promise not to sell it and keep the money for myself, but to get it to the children. I promised they would get it and they did. And that's why we did the convoy – we built a truck full of goods around the horse. For ten years, our children rocked on that horse.

That was the start of our prison story. Wheatfield gave us enormous help – many of their staff, including designers, teachers, psychologists, chefs and cleaning trainers, came out with us on their time off. These people gave us the expertise we needed to make things happen, to clean up the orphanage, to introduce better meals, better hygiene systems, all the daily grind of institutional life. They overhauled the existing system, showing us how it could be made more efficient and productive. This kind of consultancy raised the bar for many orphanages in the region. Hortolova became a centre of excellence, a showcase of good practice.

Derek shouldered the burden with us in a huge way. In Russia they presumed he was the head and I was the heart, because he was a man and so of course he must be the intelligent one! But I accepted their vision of our roles, because it was effective in getting things done and because Derek was fantastic, a superb motivator of people. His energy matched mine and he was razor-sharp. He is the world's most annoyingly positive person; painfully positive I used to tell him! In Russia most people see the glass as half empty. No matter what you tell them needs to be done, they will tell you the five hundred reasons why they can't do it. Derek was wonderful with them. I found the orphanage staff difficult in the beginning, because I was impatient and arrogant and I wanted results instantly. He explained that I had to try and motivate them in a different way. He forced us to understand things from the staff perspective, which was vital in ensuring their eventual support for what we were trying to do. There were a lot of single-stem roses bought for the women of the Russian state staff. They loved him. In fact, we made many of their dreams come true the night we bussed a large group of them to Moscow and back, to see the Bolshoi Ballet's *Swan Lake*. We booked a hotel room to get dressed up in, which I shared with twenty-two Russian women. They all changed into satin ball-gowns – no Spanx in sight! – and Derek arrived to collect us with a tiny gift for every woman. They all fell in love with him that evening. The ballet was amazing and the main beneficiaries of the trip were the children.

Derek made us all work harder, longer, better than we could have imagined. He started before us all at 6.30 a.m., no matter how cold, and worked past us all as we dropped at the end of the day. Derek never allowed any negativity on the trips and he didn't break down in the same way that the rest of us regularly did. What happened with us on those first trips would be that we would work on nuclear energy all day and then crash. We were nearly all ordinary mothers, those of us who travelled out on the early trips, and all day long we would be surrounded by small children, neglected and traumatised, usually dirty, with head lice and ringworm, who needed care so badly. There was so much to do – organising, cleaning, setting up programmes and putting systems in place, playing with these children, loving them, sometimes just sitting quietly with our arms around a tiny child who might have recently been abandoned by their mother and was still heart-broken and bewildered. It was physically exhausting and emotionally draining. By 8 or 9 o'clock at night, all any of us wanted to do was go back to the hotel where we stayed, and crash. Personally, vodka was my answer. I don't even like vodka, but I would swim in it in Russia. I understand why half the nation drinks so much of it; after twelve hours in an orphanage all I could do was try to drown what was in my head.

There were a lot of tears and a lot of people fell apart. I don't fall apart so much now, but for the first few years, it happened all the time. I would be overwhelmed and heartbroken, seeing things on a daily basis that I could never have imagined. When breakdowns happened, whoever was having one would lock themselves into an empty room somewhere for a few hours, cry it out and then, when they were ready to put back on the brave face these children needed to see, come out again and face up to the monumental task we were engaged in. Mending broken windows, doors, roofs and lives.

5

GUARDIAN ANGELS AND MEN OF IRON

The initial snowball that started rolling down the hill after *Kenny Live* and the *Sunday Independent* article, picked up volunteers along the way, incredible people who gave so much more than time. To have touched off them in my life has been an extraordinary privilege.

Jean McCarthy's was the first phone call I got after *Kenny Live*. She was a nurse from Cork, who dedicated part of the next ten years of her life to our children. Because she was a nurse and a mother, she had everything we needed. But we didn't just seek out people who had professional backgrounds. We wanted wonderful, responsible, caring people, because our approach, from day one, was that these children needed unconditional love and patience, as much as they needed doctors, dentists and psychologists. We also chose some excellent young social workers for their loving spirit and sense of fun, rather than parental expertise.

It took years, really, to start to see a profound change in the children. Whatever the ditzy daytime TV presenters would have you believe, you cannot go into an orphanage, rebuild it in twenty-four hours, throw a bucket of paint over everything, give out a few teddy bears and hope to make a lasting difference. It absolutely doesn't work. It takes a huge amount of work to make a real impact.

We never made much of an impact on the residents who were quite grown up when we arrived. They left shortly afterwards and their lives were only slightly improved. The ones who were little when we first came, who were six or so, are our most successful children, because they have received the most love, attention and money. It's not rocket science. To fix children, you need time, resources and fantastic people. Those of our children who have gone on to university or technical school, or have qualified as skilled craftsmen, or have successfully married and had children of their own – these are the ones we have had the most time with and the ones who have benefited from the full extent of our programmes.

And in truth, we couldn't have put more hours or effort into doing this. We felt the children deserved every single drop of energy we could put into them, even when we ourselves were dropping with exhaustion and completely over-emotional. When members of the core team weren't there, our incredible carers, who would go out on three-month volunteer programmes, did it for us. These carers came from all over the country and from every kind of background. They all did their final interview with Ger Ashmore, one of the directors, and me, and were subject to police checks, all of which was time-consuming. Plus they had to fund-raise to cover their own costs of getting there, so it took the best part of a year to set all of that up. Some of our carers might have been going out because they had reached some kind of crossroads or trauma in their life – they had broken up with a boyfriend maybe, or a parent had died – and three months in an orphanage seemed a good way of re-evaluating where they were. A bit of an *Eat, Pray, Love* thing. But most simply wanted to look after abandoned children.

We had to be very careful that they were well prepared for what they were getting themselves into. We needed to find people who would live in a grotty old flat in the boy's block of a freezing orphanage, who would put up with grim conditions – skinny, hard beds, cockroaches, temperatures of minus 25°C outside and no hot water in the shower. The carers' job description was simply TLC. They were not there to teach, to feed or to run the orphanage. The state staff continued to do all these things on a daily basis. Our carers were there to love the children, to play with them, to show them the kind of care they had never known. They had to be self-motivating, because we didn't give them a structure. They had to be able to get up in the morning and do whatever the day demanded and the children needed. If some child wanted to sit quietly beside you and hold your hand for an hour, your job was to be there. Not everybody can do that. You have to see the value in it. Some people want to be knitting, cleaning, keeping busy, whatever. But in Hortolova, they had to take their lead from the children – play football, sing, read, draw; whatever was wanted. We would see these carers coming for their interview looking fabulously glamorous, and the next time you'd see them they would be in the orphanage, wearing layers of cheap clothes, no make-up and not a GHD hair straightener in sight, with manky old boots ruined by snow, wet, mud and football. It was a wonderful contrast.

Once they began going out, it was like sprinkling fairy dust on the place. Before that, when I was there and it came time for us to leave the orphanage, which was always at night, about 11.30 p.m., the kids would come out, in the freezing cold, in pyjamas and try to block the road to stop us going. They would be crying, holding our hands, pulling us back, the state staff would have to come out after them and prise them loose from us. It was devastating every time. Harrowing. Because so many people come and go in their lives, they never believed we'd be back. I hated leaving them. No matter how much we swore that we were coming back, they didn't believe it. Once we got the Irish carers in place and a core team of

Russian staff selected and employed directly by To Russia With Love, the kids could relax. They didn't care about us leaving then, because they had people there who stayed, who were consistent. They finally began to understand that we meant it when we said we were going to stay.

Once the volunteer programme was up and running, we had three or four carers going out every twelve weeks and changing over with the team already there. It was a huge amount of maintenance – they lost their passports, got sick, got homesick, couldn't take any more cold water in the showers. Whatever it was, I was their link, so they would ring me if they were having a bad moment. They also rang if they had concerns about the children, any kind of bullying or abuse. Anything they saw that they didn't like, five seconds later I would know about it.

For example, if there was no petrol for the bus so the kids couldn't go anywhere, if they weren't being allowed to use the equipment we'd brought them, whatever it was, I'd hear about it instantly. Russia is three hours ahead of Ireland, so at 5 a.m. our time, it's 8 a.m. there, and that's when the calls would start to come through. I generally get up at 5 a.m. anyway, so it worked quite well. But I had to manage that carefully. Older, Soviet Russians, raised in a different system, can be paranoid about westerners, and I couldn't let them think these people were spies. I had to be very careful about how I used the information. Once we gained the respect of the staff and they realised we weren't doing it in a bitchy, malicious way, but only to improve the level of care, it became easier.

There were five or six carers living in the orphanage flat at any one time and all day long all they heard at the door was 'knock, knock, knock'. It's still like that. We have around 200 children and they will always find a reason to knock for the Irish. You might be having a quick tea break and the next thing, 'knock knock', and some little kid is standing there, sometimes without any real reason. They'd make something up – 'I need a pencil, a plaster', anything at all. Or they'd forget what they wanted as the door opened, overwhelmed simply by the need for company. For eighteen hours a day, it never ceases.

We had stringent rules about who could go where and do what. There had to be two carers everywhere and nobody was allowed into a child's room on their own. In fairness, it's impossible to fully enforce that, but those were the rules for the Irish. The carers were allowed into our flat in town once a week to let off steam. This flat was bought thanks to a one-off donation of €5,000, to which we added another €8,000; it has more than paid for itself over many years in which it has been our base: somewhere to gather, debrief, escape from outbreaks of ringworm and eat noodles off the ironing board we use as a dining-room table to this day.

How do I adequately thank all those who helped us make the dreams of countless children come true? It is an impossible task to mention all those who so willingly gave their time and energy. How can I describe all the undocumented acts of kindness to so many by so few? To you all, and for all that you did, here are some words that one of our carers wrote:

If you helped them on their journey,
If you helped them carry their load,
If you helped to lower their hill,
If you helped to level their road,
If you were one of these strangers,
And if you left your mark,
Then be so proud of your effort,
You were a candle in their dark.

Over the years, we have had some truly extraordinary people who have helped us and changed the children's lives. What follows is a selection chosen at random from among the many wonderful volunteers.

Máirtín Ó Dubhghaill from Inverin in Galway is an incredible man, a born teacher and a big gentle giant whom the children adore. There are no sides to him, he is just cut out of the land, a man of iron and it's an honour for me to have ever been in his life.

Máirtín rang me after *Kenny Live* and said, 'I'd like to help with those children, and I will get my school to help.' He was a teacher at St Patrick's Boys' School in County Galway, so he gathered together his boys, dressed them up in tinsel wings and white frocks, and for fourteen years those children have been singing in Galway's Eyre Square every year for us. They raise between €4,000 and €5,000 every year. Máirtín has the guitar out and nobody gets past him without putting something in that bucket! He and the people of Inverin have raised serious money for To Russia With Love, more than any other organisation in Ireland, well over €100,000 in ten years. He does swims on Christmas Day, auctions, raffles, bucket rattles, bag packs; anything he can do, he does. And thanks to Máirtín, every year in Tigh Mholly, this tiny gorgeous pub in Spiddal, they have a To Russia With Love night, with all proceeds going to the charity. The walls are covered with pictures of our children, and there is a real bond between the people of that small Gaeltacht area and the children of Russia.

Three or four times a year, Máirtín goes out to the orphanage and is just magic with the children. He has six of his own – all beautiful and ridiculously talented – they sing and play instruments – the type of children who make you regret not forcing your own to play an instrument. He has built playgrounds for us and painted walls, but in general he just plays the guitar every day for the endless circle of children that surround him. He has them speaking Irish – even the ones that can't speak English have a few words of Irish. Our bigger boys treat Máirtín like the dad they should have had.

He's retired now from teaching and in 2011 TG4 included him in a six-part documentary about six remarkable people from Connemara, and followed him out to Hortolova on the plane and train to watch him spending the people of Inverin's money. He carried over with him a patchwork quilt made by the children of another little school in Connemara, Scoil Naisiunta Cholmcille, where his wife is the principal, and our kids hung it in the playroom in Hortolova. Then they made something similar, though not as fancy, and sent it back. These kinds of links are really what make them believe in themselves and believe that there are people outside the walls of their orphanage who care. Connemara and certainly Inverin may be small, but the people there could teach us all a few things. They are an incredible community.

Ciara Roberts, another angel, is a force of nature. Her mammy was worried she wouldn't be able to get tea in Russia, so packed boxes of Barry's for her. If Russia ever needs a battery for their nuclear plants, Ciara is it. She cleaned endlessly, if you stood still you got scrubbed! She decorated, painted, hung curtains, made rounds of toast every night for all the big boys on the corridor, mammied the kids and all of us. Every morning she marched over to the medical block and forced the grumpy nurse to weigh her in, as part of her own home-grown Russian Weight Watchers club.

Ciaran Sweeney, teacher, designer and art class guru, froze

his eyelashes off in minus 32°C. He arrived in his daddy's woolly jumper. Ten days, many painted faces and art classes later, he left, still wearing it. In fact, he never took it off in between.

When Evelyn Forde arrived for her interview, my first thought was, 'Not a chance. Heels too high, too designer, too high-powered', but she convinced me and I'm so glad she did. This is an extract from the report she wrote back to the people who sponsored her to go out. It will give you an insight into the calibre of carer we send out:

Tuesday, 21 March 2006

'If we crash, can I eat you?' asks the man next to me in seat 12B.

'Only with a nice Chianti!' I reply. It is my first encounter with dark Russian humour …

Friday, 24 March 2006

I haven't showered since leaving Ireland, my bags have still not arrived, it is -10 degrees, I have lost count of how many times my ass has hit the ground (courtesy of industrial strength ice and the ridiculous heels I am wearing), I haven't a clue what people are saying to me, I am in a freaking forest for God's sake! And so why do I love it here?

Because I have been hugged to near death by the kids, mothered like a baby by the 'To Russia With Love' staff, welcomed with open arms by the orphanage employees and made to feel like a native by the locals …

Take 'sticker fanatic' Sergey, aged seven, for example. Every morning at 7.30 a.m., he initiates negotiations. He will co-operate in the 'getting up, dressed, breakfast and walk to school' ritual if I part with three football stickers. I counter-offer with one sticker on Sunday. Giving me a look you could spread on a sponge cake, he begs for two stickers after school today …

Sometimes, however, Sergey is not so easily appeased and without warning, his shrill shouts, uncontrollable sobs and nightmares betray a tragic pre-Hortolovan life. Who knows what horrors still cloud the head of this beautiful child who was witness to the death of his mother at the hands of an alcoholic father. The orphanage psychologist works tirelessly with Sergey (but also has to care for 134 other kids whose parents have also been deemed unfit due to neglect, alcohol/drug abuse or financial hardship). His sister is in another orphanage 300 km away. His relatives exist below the poverty line – that's the Bryansk poverty line, which is as low as you can draw a line without falling over.

Sunday, 16 April 2006

'Roma, sit down, wait until the mini-bus stops, tie up your coat, you'll get drenched,' I half stutter in pigeon Russian and half mime in English.

He's not listening, he is too excited. He last saw his brother a year ago – he is now fifty yards away and can't wait any longer.

Staradub is the polar opposite of Hortolova. It is grey, cold and impersonal. The play areas outside are empty. Dull sounds echo in the hallways – no music, no running, no laughing. The kids are wearing their coats inside and stare vacantly ... I can only hope 'To Russia With Love' get the funds it needs to 'Hortolovarise' this place.

3 June 2006

I leap up in a mild panic, hasten to the exit knocking passengers with my shopping as I pass and spring Peter Pan-like onto the quasi-platform just as the train pulls out. Within seconds, I am surrounded by kids wanting to carry my shopping through the woods ... It's a beautiful day, no one is fighting for their turn on the two bikes or five pairs of rollerblades. A ball hits me on the hand and football-mad Kolya races over, blows on it and kisses it better. I sit on the swing, swat a mosquito with deadly accuracy (I am convinced every blood-sucking insect from here to Shanghai holidays in Hortolova) and enjoy a hiccup of silence. I don't ever want to leave.

Noreen Lyons is another huge part of our story. She's the woman who came to my house all those years ago when I first came back from Hortolova. She knocked on my door in Clontarf, and said, 'Let's have a cake sale.' I had never met her before, but I said, 'OK, only I can't bake ...'

'I can,' she responded. And did. She arrived with hundreds of cakes, which we sold, and the ball began to roll.

Noreen took on an incredibly important role within To Russia With Love. She set up and ran our family sponsorship programme for fourteen years. And it was bloody hard work. She and her husband, Fergus, have a spreadsheet going back fourteen years, detailing every single child from our orphanage and some of the most amazing families in Ireland who sponsored them. The programme consisted of sponsor families who donated €200 a year and, maybe more importantly, wrote to the children: letters, birthday cards, Christmas cards, back and forth to Russia, all year long. It was a high-intensive labour of love, to get thousands of letters every year back and forth. And every single letter had to be translated. It was a horrendous job, and I doubt that anybody on this planet could have done it except Noreen. Some sponsor families were really good about writing, while others weren't as vigilant, but Noreen wouldn't let a parcel full of letters go until she was sure that every child in the orphanage was getting something.

Sadly, because of staff cutbacks, we no longer run this programme. It's such a pity, because our children adored the letters. They would wait for them, and all had a photo of their sponsor families beside their beds. When we went in and said goodnight to them, they would tell us all about how so-and-so got a new cat, or a car, or something. Often, they had never met these sponsor families, in fact, mostly they had never met them, but they felt loved by them. The kids would write back and tell the families about their birthday gift, school or new haircut. It was very simple stuff, but a strong link, one they were very proud of.

One of the first people to join that programme was Margaret Driver, who rang Noreen and asked to sponsor a child. Then she sponsored two, then three and then six. The rest of her family sponsored children too. Margaret used to write the most beautiful letters to me, about the work we were doing. One of our difficult children, Lena, was one of her charges, and Margaret used to write to her endlessly, cheering her on and just chatting to her. We all adored her.

Tragically Margaret passed away too young. When she was dying she wrote to us and the letter was read out at her funeral, about the work we were doing and the children whose lives were being changed because of it. She mentioned us all individually. It was heartbreaking. Her husband requested no flowers at the funeral, just donations to the charity. Margaret was flower-mad and had the most magnificent garden, so, from the donated money, we built a beautiful greenhouse in Hortolova in her name, and all our children go in for horticultural lessons every day. It's a huge, state-of-the-art greenhouse, with a photo of Margaret on the wall. It is a space that the weaker, shyer children love; orphanage life can be chaotic. Her husband still supports us, her daughter sends in a direct debit every month and carries the torch that Margaret lit. They are an amazing family – one of hundreds of Noreen's wonderful sponsor families.

It hasn't all been worthy, character-building stuff though. Over the years we have sent a magician, the sexiest magician ever – Etienne Pradier – to entertain the children. Etienne has always performed at our balls and it doesn't get better than him. One year a donor paid for him to go to Russia, and what a trip it was! It's not just that he is eye candy and has the sexiest French accent ever – his magic is stunning. The children were awed. Eggs were popping out of their noses, rings appearing on fingers. I watched Etienne having a Russian meltdown moment when a dotey little girl with cancer asked him to make her hair grow back.

Jerome Westbrooks, my son's African-American basketball coach, who gave his time to our children, arrived into our forest and uncurled all 6 feet 7 inches of himself from a Lada. The children were stunned, they had never seen a black person before. Jerome is a special, gifted man – he started their basketball camps and the children still play at competition level today. Jerome really left his mark. One little girl asked him did the black go all the way up as she peeped up his long shorts! He started a trend and many basketballers arrived after him – Trisha McGrath's children Jenny, Sarah and Steven, my own son, Mikey, and his friends ran sports camps. Jerome's own children got involved, and our Russian children went from zero to hero with all the attention. There are now many cups and trophies lining their walls.

Joe and Vyvienne Bell are my personal hairdressers (!) and were part of the original Christmas Santa trip, where they played the role of elves and fund-raisers. We designed this as a fund-raiser, to harness the goodwill of the many people who wanted to raise money for us. Every year we put together a group at Christmas time, everyone dresses as elves, with one man playing Santa. We visit many orphanages and distribute sacks of goodies. It's a win-win – the children are delighted and the kind volunteers feel they have truly taken part in something wonderful. More importantly, Joe and Vyvienne are also members of our two-family exclusive, members-only X Factor club. The 'club' has been running for eight years and our two families gather to watch the show at each other's houses. We do Chinese or cook, and talk all night, although the rules say no talking. We never miss it. Viv is a terrific hostess, cooks for me every time I return and calms her husband as he gets panicked over golf Gold Classics, speeches and other fund-raising matters.

All of these people are part of the magnificent tapestry that is To Russia With Love.

Not all of our guardian angels were humanitarians. Some were hardheaded businessmen, like John Patchell, who set up our Leaver's Programme and ran it for three years. He and his wife, again motivated by *Kenny Live*, sponsored two of our children, a little girl called Oxana and a boy called Ruslan. When it came time for Ruslan to leave the orphanage, because he was too old for it, John, who is a very successful businessman, decided I wasn't doing enough for the leavers – he was right, I wasn't, I was mostly minding the ones on the inside. John was very dedicated to Ruslan's class, who were all school-leavers, and set up a programme for them to help them get through third level education and support them in making careers for themselves. Now, John, although a compassionate man, wanted to concentrate on those children who wanted to help themselves. He criticised me many times because he felt I was trying to mind too many. His thinking was, 'You can't save them all, much as we would like to, so you concentrate on the strong.' He's probably right, although I would never tell him that! But I would always have wanted to stick by the weaker ones, the ones who hadn't a chance without us.

John visited colleges, universities and third level schools around Russia, paving the way for our orphans. He never paid a bribe (accepted practice in some places), though he did bring in plenty of bottles of whiskey and many boxes of Irish chocolates, and ran a truly super programme.

John interviewed the children one by one and selected this team of 'diamonds' as we called them – our really, really strong candidates. He committed himself to three years of a programme mentoring them, finding accommodation, meeting their teachers and generally smoothing their path, and was as good as his word. Though the three years are up, he stays in touch with the boys – they were all boys in that class – who are constantly on Skype to him. It's like he has a family of big sons to add to his two at home. He is a wonderful man, and a role model, who has changed the lives of many children.

One of the boys he supported was Slava, still among our greatest success stories – all the more so because for a long time I feared he would end up with a knife in his back somewhere. He was a dark-natured child, deep, difficult and too good-looking for his own good. We'd had him since he was small. His mother abandoned him when he was four and died about three years ago. He has a sister who is very good to him now, but he didn't see her for ten years while he was in the orphanage. He was always one of our more troublesome boys, bright, but undisciplined, and didn't know what he wanted to do with himself. Then John Patchell put him through law college, monitored him, nurtured him, mentored him and chastised him many times because he wasn't working hard enough and was capable of more than he was doing.

Once he graduated as a lawyer, Slava went to work for a big Russian bank. Recently he got married and has a wonderful mother-in-law, a dressmaker who makes ball-gowns for all our girls when they graduate. He is one of the first children to go back into the orphanage on a regular basis and help the younger ones. It would be fantastic if that could happen more often, but it won't. Our grown-up kids are still fighting to survive themselves. They don't have money to give back to the orphanage and they probably never will have in the world they live in. Slava is incredibly grateful to the Irish and to Hortolova for all they have done for him. He was in Ireland a few years ago, he gave a talk at the Four Seasons hotel in Dublin about his life and what it had meant to him to be cared for by To Russia With Love. He thanked the audience and the Irish for replacing the parents that had abandoned all these children. There truly wasn't a dry eye in the house.

Our staff in Russia deserve even more credit than any of the volunteers. We couldn't begin to pay them what they're worth; in fact, they work incredibly hard for minimal financial reward. Truly, they aren't in it for the money. I'm always conscious that we overwork them and expect them to handle every situation, from funerals to the buying of 1,000 Santa gifts. It is hard to do justice to these staff when describing them: the beautiful, soft, angelic Inna, a mama to so many; Olga, programme director, friend, mentor to our single mums, minder in detention centres, cooker of all the dinners in our children's flats, Russian mum to my own kids; Zhenya, my adviser, a role model to a decade of boys, a friend, and a trusted member of the To Russia With Love family; Sasha, a quiet, stoic, shy young man, who minds our boys daily and has the awful job of shopping, and fixing bikes, PCs and rollerblades; Oksana, a gorgeous nurse, minder, mentor to many; Olga II, designer of the playroom and mother to all our smallest ones; Alla, our first employee, who started on €10 a month in 1998; Tanya, Ira, Julia, Natasha, Losha, Vasya, Lena, Sveta and all the wonderful Russians who have given so much to the children over the years and still do to this day. I doubt we know the half of it. We are so lucky with our staff. Currently we have six people fronting all of our programmes in Russia, with me and two part-timers in the Dublin office.

All of these people, Irish and Russian, kept my batteries charged over the years and they are another reason why I fight on. My apologies to those I have not named, I simply cannot list everyone, but the children know you and love you and that's really all that matters.

6

OF FUND-RAISING
AND EXTORTION

Back home in Ireland, we were rapidly turning into event managers as the Celtic Tiger took off and the country's super-rich showed themselves willing to pour huge sums of money into charities, as long as they were given the right kind of encouragement.

In the very early days, the kind of cash-splashing was unbelievable – I'll never forget one lunch, men only except for a couple of us girls, all stockbrokers, some of whom had flown in from London just for the day. These guys were high on the amounts of money they were making, they were also drinking merrily and had decided to support us. They were betting each other crazy sums, to do crazy things. One guy had a comb-over and someone was bet a wad of cash to snip it off. When he did it, he won €5,000, which went straight to us. I know that sounds really macho and over the top, but their generosity was really extraordinary. You could make €30,000 to €40,000 in one lunch session. Now, that all petered out after the very early days and we had to be more structured in our approach to raising funds, but in the beginning, there seemed to be no end to the flood of donations.

To Russia With Love ran about twenty events a year, everything from ladies lunches or golf classics, to walks in exotic places like Machu Picchu, the Great Wall of China and the Pyramids. Each event had a different committee behind it, although I was involved in how everything was run. Julie Hogan, followed by Joanna Fortune, ran a tight ship in the office – these two fabulous women brought so much to To Russia With Love. The highlight of the calendar was undoubtedly the annual ball. Back then, balls were the big thing, everyone wanted to get dressed up and wear a king's ransom worth of diamonds. I doubt whether you could give away tickets in the current climate; balls are simply not the thing any more! In order to stand out from the crowd of events, we wanted ours to be a really gorgeous, high-end event, and I think we consistently achieved that, thanks to our very glam and razor-sharp Ball Committee, a fabulous bunch of sexy, committed, organised women, headed up by a lifelong friend, Brenda O'Connell.

The *Sunday Independent* continued to be very supportive and always carried photographs and a social piece on who was there, who wore what, spent what and so on. Mary O'Sullivan was wonderful at twisting her colleagues' arms – she sent Gayle Killilea to cover the very first ball we did, in the days before Gayle married Sean Dunne and became someone who attended the balls rather than wrote about them. Barry Egan has helped for fourteen years by getting us fantastic prizes for auction – dinner cooked by the ever-generous Neven Maguire in your own kitchen, or a bedroom makeover by my wonderful friend, designer Ciaran Sweeney, for example. Brendan O'Connor would MC and have the room rolling around with his description of his days as a child in Soviet Russia, living on the streets after the Bolshoi ballet dumped him, before I rescued him. Artist Pauline Bewick gave us a painting every year for eleven years, to be auctioned. And every year the same person bought her painting, bidding about €5,000 in order to get it. Marian Keyes did the auction for us one year after her trip to the orphanage, because we specifically wanted toys for the kids for Christmas, and she got it up to €30,000, which was just amazing.

Each year that ball raised about €150,000. We would have no money at all walking in the door, even though we always sold out every table in advance. Each ticket cost €200, but that would have been long spent on hire of the room, the meal and the champagne, which was all paid for up front, and no, the hotels didn't give any kind of discount because we were a charity. As a result, all our money had to come from the raffle and the auction on the night. We always had incredibly successful auctions, but even so, every year we went in sweating, flat broke and totally dependent on the kind of excitement and goodwill we could generate.

Every year we had to have a really sexy idea, to raise the cash. That meant buying *Hello!* magazine, checking out what had been done at the Marbella ball for example, and documenting it for the following year. Whatever was being done around the world, we were copying it immediately, so we always had really fab balls, with make-up artists in the toilets and magician Etienne Pradier, who came over from the UK. Frankly, if Etienne pulled a dead rabbit out of a hat we wouldn't have minded, we were all drooling. However, he was a gifted magician! We threw money at the ball, but it was always worth it, because we got it back, many times over.

At the time, fund-raising wasn't difficult. You could ask and you were given. I know all those property guys were out of control, spending and buying, but they were giving too. The charities benefited hugely, donations were being given in the millions. There was certainly a lot of ego involved – some of these guys were pitching up to the Four Seasons in a dinner jacket in order to do a bit of chest-thumping and show off to all their friends how much they could spend. However, there were also many who simply donated quietly.

Before our balls, we always sat down at a meeting with

a table plan and we knew exactly where our biggest bidders were seated, and we made sure to put our prettiest girls at that table, wearing the shortest skirts. It's a science and we worked it! The girls were there to be charming and make damn sure there was somebody there with a paddle, ready to put it straight up as soon as Mr Property Developer raised his hand, so the auctioneer didn't miss their bid. I know that sounds horribly ruthless, but we had to be horribly ruthless. And we did it in a nice way.

Sometimes, I hardly had to lift a finger for money to be pledged. I remember being in a bar one night, meeting a man and somehow telling him how frustrated I was over the new girls' block, which had just opened, but which still needed a roof. It cost €250,000 to renovate the building and the roof would have been another €50,000. We just didn't have it. He asked where I lived, I told him, and he said he'd call round to me the next day. He did, with a cheque for €48,000, raised from among a handful of his friends. The Irish had money then and the men who gave to us were all heart, even the ones who made the most noise. The plight of children always brought out their wallets and they trusted me to spend it right. I love Irish men. That's certainly the most successful I ever was at a bar …

By and large, we were rigorously ethical about where our money came from. These days, if Satan came up the office stairs with a suitcase full of money, I'd be tempted to take it!

My board might have something to say about it, but personally, I wouldn't. We have always had a harder fight, because our children are not Irish children, and that is even more so the case these days when there is so much less money around.

Those were very schizophrenic days. On the one hand, there was all this fabulousness – charity balls, dizzy sums of money being donated and endless awards. I was nominated for *Tatler* Woman of the Month, the Spirit of Ireland award and so on. *Marie Claire*, extravagantly, arrived over from London to take my picture for their Woman of the Month piece, and insisted on bringing their own make-up artist and hair stylist. I would be getting phone calls, asking me to chat on radio or appear on TV. There were weeks when I felt I was in the hairdressers all the time, getting my hair blow-dried, and at high-powered meetings constantly, from foreign affairs to EU grant meetings. For many years, the Department of Foreign Affairs in Ireland supported To Russia With Love and were a pleasure to deal with. They no longer do so because the Russian economy is now so much stronger.

Inevitably, all this fabulousness was followed by hoovering, cleaning and picking up all the stuff my wonderful family leave lying around on a daily basis. And then, every four weeks, I would get the flight to London, a connecting flight to Moscow, followed by seven hours on a train. And with every mile travelled I would shed more of Fund-raising Debbie, becoming instead Orphanage Debbie. There were days when I would be sitting out there, with a little one on my knees who had just been abandoned by her mother, on the phone to Dublin deciding whether to get the champagne for €22 or €18 a bottle for the ball. It was very surreal. Both worlds had to work together every day. It wasn't easy, but in truth I loved the adrenaline rush of it all.

On these Russian trips we stayed in a rundown hotel in the town rather than at the orphanage. The place was wall-to-wall prostitutes. The first time Mick came out to Russia with me was when Zina was ten. The Irish health board was so slow at processing her adoption that it still wasn't complete by then, which meant, under Russian law, that Zina had to come back to Russia and be interviewed by a judge about where she wanted to live. The poor child vomited the entire way from Dublin to London and from London to Moscow. She was terrified that the authorities would keep her there and not let her come home with us. On that trip, we went together to the baby orphanage where she had spent her first seven years and Zina took me by the hand to show me her little bed in the corner. It was a heartbreaking moment. After she left that orphanage, her class was moved to Hortolova.

In the event the interview went perfectly and the judge granted Zina the right to continue living with us. I was lucky to have a very good friend conveniently high up in the Federal

Security Bureau (FSB) and father of one of our beautiful Russian interpreters, Lena. He was a great protector of To Russia With Love for many years, and stood at the back of the courtroom, wearing his floor-length leather coat and giving our situation the silent seal of approval. Despite his forbidding exterior, any time we went to dinner at his home, this man always had my favourite wild strawberries, picked from his own *dacha* (wooden country house), as he knew I loved them.

Actually, I don't suppose there was ever much real doubt about the outcome of the court visit. Once again, thank God for the Russian determination to try and understand what is better for the child. So unlike the Irish, in my experience. Zina, thrilled at the verdict, went straight out and rang my mother, to tell Monny she was officially her grandmother!

Mick came too, of course, and when we got back to Dublin I noticed him standing in the bathroom, scratching like a lunatic. I could see all these tiny white things, with legs, crawling all over his body. I rang Dr Wheeler, who'd previously been with me to Russia, and told him what I'd seen. 'That sounds like crabs,' he said. 'Would Mick have been with a prostitute?'

I said, 'No, but he was in the local hotel with me.'

'Well, that's it then!' said my doctor. The hotel rented rooms by the hour and were none too careful about cleaning them between clients.

At night, after a long day in the orphanage, we'd come back to the hotel and maybe have a drink over a greasy plate of cold chips floating in disgusting oil, surrounded by prostitutes coming and going. It was gruesome and horrible, but compellingly voyeuristic in a way. You'd see some girl go upstairs with a punter and be back down in ten minutes. Or one guy would order three girls, all dressed up in matching red wigs, and they'd go off to a room together. Although we watched and commented between ourselves, we had to be very careful. The pimps were seriously intimidating, with gun handles poking out of their jacket pockets.

There was a time when everybody was watched in Russia. Every single hotel corridor had a woman sitting at the end of it, with no role except to note down who went where, when. Some hotels still have them. I don't know what their role is now. I got to know all the women at the end of our corridors and they knew what we were doing. We used to bring in gifts for them – they loved flower bulbs, so we'd bring in half a suitcase of bulbs and they'd plant them. It was necessary. If we hadn't, we couldn't have made any difference. In Russia, you need to buy goodwill, even if it is just with small, thoughtful things. If you don't keep the woman at the end of the corridor sweet, other problems arise – you end up not getting to the orphanage the next day, or somebody pulls your paperwork. This is reality and the case in all former eastern block countries. Some organisations admit it, some don't. We do.

I have had first-hand experience of the kinds of things that can happen in Russia and it can be quite scary. One night, during one of the early visits, I was taken out of my hotel room in the middle of the night by a couple of thugs. It was about 2 a.m., I was asleep, when somebody hammered on the door and began shouting at me in Russian. When I opened the door I understood just enough, from their words and especially gestures, to realise that they were insisting I go with them. There is security in hotels, but that night no security guard was there to stop these guys.

John Mulligan was in the room next door. I woke him up to explain what was happening and he said, 'I'm going with you.' We also brought our interpreter. They took us downstairs to a black van with four or five other men in it. I was naïve, indignant and concerned that I had no make-up on. If I was going to be shot, I wanted to have my Flawless Finish in place – please take note anyone who ever thinks about kidnapping me! John had hold of my arm and was saying quietly, 'Get into the back of the van and do exactly what you're told.'

We were taken to the top floor of a tower block – everybody lived in a tenement in Russia then, and this was clearly somebody's home. It was a little bit like a scene from *Goodfellas*. There were ten or twelve men around a small table, playing poker, with bottles of vodka and dense smoke everywhere. Were they mafia? Businessmen? Whoever they were, they were certainly very intimidating. One man began negotiating with our interpreter about money. I didn't know what they were saying, we were just standing there while this conversation was going on, but it was definitely threatening. In a situation like that, instead of being diplomatic, my instinct is to say, 'Well to hell with you!' John was trying to make me not do that. He was saying, 'Shut up, say nothing for now.' He was wise. I wasn't being wise, I was saying, 'No John, I don't think these men have any right to take me out of my bed at 2 o'clock in the morning …' all indignant. It wasn't smart; they could have shot us on the spot.

After the negotiations had gone on for a while, our interpreter explained that they were looking for money – €180,000. At that point, we had a plan to raise €250,000 in the first year – which we thought was a fantastic sum! The idea that I would give over half of that to these mobsters made me so furious that I ignored John's warnings, and said, 'How dare you ask me for money? The people of Ireland are giving this money for the children, and they're giving it to me in good faith. If you think I'm going to hand over a red cent to any of you gangsters …' I'm quite sure that our interpreter was not translating the full extent of it, but I think they would have known by my body language what I was saying anyway.

Eventually, they brought us back to the hotel and told me I had a week to think about it, or we would be out, that we wouldn't work in Russia again. That was it as far as sleep was concerned for the night. I didn't know how powerful these guys actually were, but my first reaction was to talk to the governor. I didn't know what else to do.

So the next morning, after a sleepless night, I went and demanded to see him. I got all teary, I was exhausted, and stunned at what had happened. Also, I believed he was a nice person, based on my previous conversations with him. And in fact he behaved very decently, told me to calm down and said he would investigate the situation on my behalf. He also guaranteed it would not happen again. He cleared the decks for me and we became quite close after that. In fact, it was the bridges I built with the Russian authorities that allowed the charity to be so successful and are what still have me there today. I have had a great relationship with the successive governors, they still send me faxes and a rose on my birthday. I was bestowed with medals, ribbons and awards, invited to dinner parties and midnight picnics, and even described as 'The Irish Scarlet O'Hara!' Russians love *Gone with the Wind* – it's still one of the biggest-selling books there – they love that indomitable, fighting spirit of Scarlet. They decided that I had something similar and because of that, I think, they let me away with a lot.

7

YOU CAN GO FOR A WALK, BUT BE BACK IN TEN MINUTES!

Igor Stepanov has been my bodyguard, protector, friend, paracetamol-supplier, shampoo-buyer and expert on all things Russian for all the years of To Russia With Love. He joined our organisation from another Chernobyl charity almost on day one, and has been a never-ending source of good sense and stern discipline ever since. Once my mother knows Igor is with me on a trip, she doesn't worry in the slightest, no matter where I'm going or what crazy thing I'm doing. He is a warm, affable character – a big cuddly Russian bear – with huge diplomacy skills. Only for him, we truly wouldn't have survived a year. Where I ranted at officials, he translated that into quiet but lethal diplomacy. He's a remarkable guy, and over the years he has come to believe strongly in what we do. He couldn't but be converted after travelling over a million miles with me.

He is without doubt one of the best interpreters I've heard

in my life. It's a remarkable skill and a lot of interpreters are useless, especially the younger ones. They will condense what you've said, reduce the meaning of it if they feel like it or, if they can, lazily use three words where you have carefully chosen ten. Igor on the other hand is a simultaneous interpreter, he listens and talks at the same time, and he is flawless. He's the perfect excuse for why my Russian is so poor!

Oh, and he's a total control freak too. Once Igor meets us at the airport, no matter how many we are or what our particular mission is, everyone has to do exactly what he says. His worst times are undoubtedly the Christmas Santa trips, because he arrives at the airport and twenty carers dressed as elves, and a couple of Santas, noisy, giddy and with scant regard for the many rules of Russia, get off the plane. But Igor rounds them up, instructions are given and woe betide anyone who doesn't follow the plan! We turn into junior infants going on a nature walk, just short of holding hands.

He organises all the money-changing. If there are vegetarians, allergies, emergencies or any other special requirements, he makes sure these needs are met. When my daughter, Sophie, first went out there as a volunteer, she was seventeen and he routinely had her tracked. He would tell me she was at the cinema, so when I was talking to her I'd ask how the film was and she'd say, 'I can't believe you knew I was at the cinema!' I loved it. She hated it.

The result is that once we see Igor, we all stop thinking. Because he minds everything. Then, when we come home, we all fall apart. We can't do anything for ourselves. I remember when I was doing Zina's adoption, Igor was handling the Russian side of it. He rang me from Russia one night to say he needed me to send him Zina's old Russian passport. I was standing in my kitchen in Dublin at the time and said, 'Oh God, where am I going to find that?' It had been months since I'd seen it. 'Get a stool, get up to the cupboard on top of your microwave, there is a folder in there and the passport is in the folder,' was Igor's answer. And sure enough, there it was. He'd obviously seen me put it up there six months previously and remembered the precise location. My family still laughs about that to this very day.

We've hardly had a fight in fifteen years – maybe cross words once (certainly I will never forget the look on his face when he discovered I had left my bag on the pavement where I had been sitting in Moscow, with €6,000 in it; thank God it was still there an hour later!) – and if I decide I want to do something, even if he disagrees with me, if I really, really push it, he will arrange everything. The minibus will be waiting at 6 a.m., or whatever time, with everything I need on it. Even so, he gives me very little rope: 'If you want to go for a walk,' he'll say, 'okay, but go in this direction and be back in ten minutes.' He says we really don't realise what's out there, how dangerous

Russia can be. We think like Irish people, not Russians.

As long as Igor is around, and as long as we all do exactly what he says, nothing can go wrong. It's only when we start to try and do our own thing that it all goes haywire ...

I was asked to speak at a really big conference in Siberia a few years ago – about 1,000 very serious Russians, all with the usual PhDs and so on, sitting staring at me as I talked to them about Ireland, charity and philanthropy. Derek Tracy was there too, talking about the prison service in Ireland and de-institutionalisation; I'd say we were the light relief! And it was initially daunting, but we met some truly amazing people. Siberia is a well-governed region, with some state-of-the-art projects, some of the best I have seen in Russia.

After the first day of the conference, we were taken to this lovely little wooden tea-house in the middle of the Siberian forest. Siberia is one of the most beautiful places on earth I'd say, with deep forests that go on for thousands of miles. But it's freezing cold. It was minus 43°C when we arrived, with a ferocious wind chill factor. You have to wear a balaclava or your face burns with the cold. Anyway, we were sitting in this hut, totally exhausted after the day, and I suggested a walk. We persuaded Igor to agree, as we were just going to go out for a couple of minutes, turn around and come back again. The sun was setting, the smell of the forest was clear and lovely, and it was all so beautiful that we just kept walking and walking. The snow was hip-deep, but there were trails in it, criss-crossing through the woods. We were leaving little bits of twigs and moss behind us, to help find our way back. We should have known it wouldn't work; it didn't work for Hansel and Gretel! It started to snow, heavily, so our moss and twigs were quickly covered. The trails get denser and denser as you go deeper into the woods, and it is impossible to retrace your steps. It was also, by then, getting dark, fast, because the sun sets very rapidly in winter in Siberia. I wasn't that scared really, because I was with Derek, and so I figured we'd somehow be all right as he is a bit of a MacGyver, but there's no doubt we were in a very serious situation. We were wrapped up in our Great Outdoors gear, but even that wasn't warm enough – fur is what you really need in that climate – and we wouldn't have survived a night.

Eventually a rescue crew arrived, found us and brought us back. And there was Igor, waiting. After twenty minutes, when we hadn't come back, he had said, 'They'll be dead by the morning', and called a crew straight away. He was furious with us, asking, 'How can you be so stupid?' We were like two naughty kids, standing in front of him. Again, the junior infant syndrome. It was funny, but we didn't dare laugh.

That was one of my first times to be let out without him and I blew it. He really didn't understand how anyone could be so irresponsible. He cannot understand how undisciplined the Irish are. He's extremely controlling, but for good reasons. He says the Irish have no notions of safety – we live in an incredibly safe country. We are not threatened by nature or, much, by society, and so we simply don't get how dangerous Russia can be, on any number of levels.

Another time I was let out without Igor was when I arrived into Moscow airport with a wonderful carer called Hilary Casey, who was on her first trip to Russia. And of course we ran into trouble.

Hilary is a kind, lovely person and a beautiful girl who has a sight problem that requires her to wear specialised glasses. At the time we were running a huge art competition among the children of all the orphanages we were involved with. A team from Ireland were coming in after us to judge the competition, and Hilary and I were going ahead in order to pick up prizes – more art materials!

Because of this, instead of taking the train as usual, a minibus, driven by Valery, our regular driver, picked us up at the airport, and Hilary and I went to Ikea first. We left late at night, the minibus filled with easels, huge rolls of paper and blackboards. Hilary and I were in the back, and one of our staff, Inna, was in the front seat with Valery. About an hour into the journey, Valery hit a patch of black ice and the bus veered into the middle of the road. There was a 40-foot container truck coming straight towards us on the other side, the road was pitch black, with fields of snow for miles to the left and miles to the right. This is *Dr Zhivago* land, a place of endless fields. Valery made a sensible decision to drive off the edge of the road rather than sit and be hit by the container truck.

All I remember is the sound of screaming. Hilary's head hit the front of my head as the minibus reached a hill and started to roll, on its side. There were no safety belts, so no one was strapped in. We were hitting the roof, the floor, the roof again, the floor again. The blackboards all came off the back seat and smashed into us. Hilary's glasses came off, hit my face and broke. By a miracle, we ended the right way up in 10 feet of snow in a field. The snow actually saved our lives because it stopped us. Inna was bleeding badly from her nose and mouth. I was fine, or sort of fine, because I had to be. The situation wasn't looking good.

We had no blankets or anything useful in the bus. Valery couldn't get it to move at all, so he left the ignition on, because it was minus 25°C and two o'clock in the morning, and set off to get help. We were all quite shocked, in fact, the two girls were in shock. Meanwhile I could smell diesel and didn't know if that was a bad thing, if it would asphyxiate us. So I rang Mick in Dublin and explained what was going on. He said to leave the ignition on, because it was so cold, and rang Igor, who rang me. Igor of course had minded me for about ten years by then and nothing had happened. The one time he didn't come and collect me, look what happened! Not that he said that. He just got on with fixing the situation.

An ambulance arrived after about an hour and then a tow-truck. They roped the minibus up, and we all sat in it and got pulled back to the orphanage, a journey of seven hours because we had to move so slowly. No windscreen, a badly smashed-in roof, no lights and all of us girlies rather stunned.

It wasn't fun at all. And the next morning I had to be up, high heels, suit on, to judge this art competition. We had 500–600 children arriving for it, all excited. I had to just get on with it and so I did. Hilary was still in shock, it took her a couple of days to get herself together and decide to stay, but in the end she did, and she was one of our best carers. Because of her own sight condition, she had a very strong bond with the blind orphanage we were involved with. She took that on as her personal project and visited regularly. Once back in Ireland, she contacted the National Council for the Blind, and they started collecting money and sending out lovely equipment to the children, such as balls with a tiny bell in the middle so they could follow the sound and play catch or football. It's a simple idea, but the equipment is very expensive, and those children would never have got it if it hadn't been for Hilary and the generosity of the National Council for the Blind.

Igor often has great difficulty with the Irish sense of humour. Things that are hysterical to us just don't strike him as funny at all. Like the time Gordon Dooley, our Santa on one Christmas trip, decided to roll up a kilometre of hotel carpet, wearing only his underpants and singing *Jingle Bells* at 4 a.m. Now, the particular hotel we stayed in on that trip is seriously bling – the lights even have a disco setting. On the wall was a huge landscape painting of a naked woman in lace. I'd say it cost €9.99 in the local market, but it was impressive. One of our elves took it off the wall and laid it in his bed, joking that it was the closest he was going to get to a Russian woman. We all thought it was hysterical. Igor didn't think it was funny at all. Then the woman in the corridor – who's only job it is to watch what goes on, who goes where and does what, called him and asked why the painting was gone. Russians are so disciplined. They would never do anything like that. Neither Igor nor the lady could begin to understand that this was funny. At such times, I can see that for all the years he has spent working so closely with us, Igor is still very much a Russian man!

That said, he now understands me like no one else. He minds us to death; we have never had anyone lost or had trouble in fourteen years because of him. In 2010 I won a UNESCO Tolerance award, which was lovely but made those around me laugh. We all agreed that if anyone deserved it, it was Igor. He truly has been the cog in the machine it all pivots on and we love each other deeply.

8

SO MANY STORIES

My life had become a huge balancing act. In Dublin I was managing a board and was directly involved in planning all the events, while in Russia I was managing the situation with the administrators and in the orphanages themselves I was managing the building meetings and the many development programmes (see Appendix A) that were growing so successfully.

I've sat through more building meetings than I care to dwell on and, mother of Jesus, they were the most painful things! Russians are really funny, you never know who is at the table because no one ever introduces anyone. You go into a room where there are seventeen people all wearing fur hats – they love huge meetings, because everything seems very important then – and some man will talk for twenty minutes, only for it to turn out that he's the driver for one of them, but felt he had an opinion about the toilets or the pipes, or whatever was under discussion.

Mobile phones were new and very important back then, so

you'd have seventeen people in the room and everybody's phone would be ringing. No matter who it was, they always took the call, even if it was their wife asking, 'Do you want borscht for dinner?' They roared down the phone. It was highly disruptive and truly hilarious. On one occasion a woman was wearing what was clearly a brand-new pair of glasses. In Russia, they like you to know when they have something new – and we knew, because she'd left the price tag on the actual glass bit. Every time one of the Irish would catch someone else's eye, they would dissolve into hysterics. A couple of times people had to leave the room, under the pretext of a toilet break or a coughing fit, because they couldn't hold it together.

Actually, many things about those meetings were hilarious, even if in a very grim kind of way. I remember any number of intense discussions about sanitary towels, for example. The famous old regulations, again, that couldn't be tampered with, didn't specify any kind of budget for sanitary towels, because such things barely existed then, and so, of course, in 2001 sanitary towels were still deemed, officially, not to exist. All the orphan girls would just cut up cloth and old blouses to make rags. I was determined to get them something better – as far as I'm concerned, dignity is vital!

But sitting in a meeting with an orphanage director who has never discussed any women's issues in his entire life, let alone something so intimate, and demanding a budget for sanitary towels, was just hilarious. These budgets were set by the Department of Education in Bryansk and they determined what everything was spent on. Our input was to top-up inadequate budgets – i.e., pay the difference between plastic shoes and leather shoes – or fill gaps where we found them. Sanitary towels were just such a gap. For a year, non-stop, we had the sanitary towel conversation, until at one point I remember Igor saying, 'I cannot translate that word one more time!' Try explaining to a big, macho Russian man why these things are necessary – the words were getting stuck in everyone's throat. We really needed a drink at the end of those days!

The building meetings were pretty similar. We had appointed the children as our interior designers – we allowed them to choose the colours of paint and tiles, and they chose pink – proper, bright, sugar-plum pink. But no, we were told, you can't have pink. You can only have mint green or magnolia or nasty brown, because those are the colours specified by Stalin's stylist I think! It was immensely tedious stuff and the only thing to do was keep asking, keep insisting, until we eventually broke them down. It's not easy to break Russians down, but if there's one thing I can do, it's talk forever; eventually, I wore them out. And it was worth it, just to see the look on the children's faces when the buckets of pink paint first arrived.

And those at the meetings didn't always like it. On the day the ribbon was cut on our first building – an ancient building that we had gutted and renovated – on a point of principle, none of the architects would come along. It was sugar-plum pink, with big sunny arch-shaped, double-glazed white windows – designed with tender loving care by our own children. Stalin must have been spinning in his grave.

There was so much practical stuff to be done, so much renovating and rebuilding and cleaning and mending, that at times it was hard to remember the other side of our mission – to love the children. To show them kindness, affection and respect, to try and build their self-esteem, something that is in very short supply with orphan children. To try and foster this, as well as proper bedrooms, clean new bathrooms and so on, we built something that I called the suitcase room.

We had spotted the children going up and down a rickety ladder to the manky old attic. One day I went up to see what they were doing and found a room wedged full of ancient old suitcases, mostly made out of battered cardboard. The children were like mice, scrabbling round the suitcases, so I asked, 'What is this room?' It turned out that when the children first arrived at the orphanage, they brought with them a suitcase, which was then taken from them. They could have had an old pair of shoes in the case, or possibly a photo of their mother, or even a letter. The suitcases were treasure trunks for

these children, the only link with family and early life, but
they were just dumped in the attic, one on top of the other,
in great heaps. It was filthy, freezing and wet up there, with
water running down the walls and snow falling through the
broken roof. And yet these children would spend their time up
there, hunting through the piles to find their own memories.
Clearly, these suitcases were just the most precious things in
the world to them. So when we renovated, we built a suitcase
room. Now, they all have their own spot, on nice white shelves,
with sliding ladders so they can reach their suitcase. We have
tables where they can sit and go through it all. I felt it was very
important to them to be able to do that.

There was a lady who looked after that room, who just sat
there in the corner, looking like she was going to kill us. When
they don't know you, Russians have that look down to a fine
art – it's hilarious. Previous to the rebuild, it was wet, freezing
and miserable for her there too, and she had nothing to while
away the time – no kettle, no cup. So we bought her a kettle
and suddenly she was a different person. It was like we had
given her a company car. Small things, as we discovered, could
make such a huge difference.

To be honest, in the beginning, I didn't think about the staff
at all, I just thought about the children. But actually, you have
to think about the staff. There's no point giving the children a
magnificent suitcase room, or rollerblades, or a playground, if

the woman minding them doesn't have a cup of tea to have a break in a twelve-hour shift. So we put in a staff room, with a TV in it, and beautiful cups and saucers. We budgeted for a supply of cakes and biscuits every Friday. Overnight, the staff went from being dour and hostile to being pleasant and helpful. Basically, 'management' in Russia often simply means treating people indifferently. Russian bosses have a lot to learn in the area of people motivation. We started to get under the skin of why Russians look so miserable all the time. We have been lucky in Hortolova to work with many wonderful state staff, who have helped us, welcomed us and been there for the children when we were not. It took time to befriend them, but a little respect goes a long way – they eventually became our allies.

We discovered pretty quickly that children in orphanages aren't allowed birthday parties, because there are too many of them. Then one day I opened a door and discovered a tiny little old babushka, a wonderful old woman who was like a grandmother to some of our children, and she had six of them in there with her and was pouring them all a cup of tea from a samovar. The children were tiny and all looked up at me, terror-struck because I'd caught them. The babushka apologised, saying, 'I'm so sorry, we're not allowed to have birthday parties, I knew I'd be in trouble if I got caught but ...' The very next morning we started a birthday party programme.

In the Dublin office, we have all the children's names on the wall, with their birth dates, and they are all bought a present. We have one party a month, for all the children born in that month, because there really are too many to celebrate each birthday individually.

Once they reach sixteen, they go out for pizza and coke. Before us, they weren't allowed out, ever. Even now I notice that they treasure the empty pizza box, on their shelf or under their beds, for months afterwards.

At one stage, we bought six pairs of football boots for the boys' team. In the early days, people regularly left items on the doorstep of our office in Dublin for the children and somebody had donated these new boots. At their next match, the boys turned up, all wearing one boot each, and one normal shoe, so that everyone got a boot. After that we went out and spent a fortune on sports gear for them and, amazingly, they started winning everything. They would get off the bus, feeling great, and play a terrific match. Before, they would have felt totally inferior to the family children of the rival teams, which knocked their confidence so much that they always lost.

After a couple of years, when word about what we were doing at Hortolova spread, occasionally children would run away from other orphanages and come to us. We had to send them back, which was heartbreaking, but there was nothing else we could do. Many of them would be siblings of our own children – a brother or sister would arrive at the railings, having heard what life was like at Hortolova. We might do our best to keep them, but orphanages are organised in a very rigid way.

Actually, it's an insane system. The day a child is taken from their parents, or given up, they are put through an academic assessment – asked questions, such as 'What is a peninsula?' to a seven-year-old. None of my three children in Ireland could have answered that question at that age. Based on their response to many such questions, they are attributed an academic level and dispatched to the relevant orphanage. Once there, they are almost never reassessed. In my fourteen years I've seen two or three reassessed, because it was so shockingly obvious that they were too bright for their situation. But normally that doesn't happen and generally the bright child will eventually give up the fight and sink to the level around them.

In 'slow-learner' orphanages, there are only a small number of trades open to the children when they leave – the girls can be brick-layers or plasterers, the boys can mix cement. They rarely qualify for anything else. After all, there are gazillions of industrial jobs that need to be filled – farm labourers, brick-layers and so on. The system needs those numbers coming out to sustain them.

Even though the Russian side of it was desperately hard, it was also incredibly heady and addictive. I have a life coach who gives me his time a few times a year and he says, 'You couldn't go for a walk unless you had stones in your shoes.' For some reason, I need the hard stuff. If it's easy, it bores me instantly. And so I stuck it out, through all the challenges, until we reached a new phase when we began to expand the charity, taking on more orphanages and children.

Russia is full of stories. Most are hard-luck stories. Or at least, the ones I heard were. But word got around very quickly, that there was a bunch of crazy Irish about who had nothing better to do with their money than give it to orphans. And so people began to seek me out. They would wait for me outside my hotel, telling me about their nephew who needed an operation, their granny who needed a wheelchair, someone else who needed to be buried, or a headstone. The stories were endless. At conferences that I was invited to attend, or to speak at, other orphanage directors would have me pointed out to them and would beg me to look at their kitchens or bathrooms. We said no to most requests.

Yet we couldn't ignore all the stories. As the money built in Ireland, and as we got stronger as an organisation, we had too much money for Hortolova. It wasn't right that one group of children was getting so much, while others had nothing. It was unfair. By the time our children had a playground, decent shoes and the opportunity to visit siblings, we began to feel we needed to look around. Yes, we could have done

126

loads more for them, bought them all computers and iPads and laptops, but when the orphanage down the road has no shoes, it doesn't feel right. Hortolova isn't Disneyland, but it is gorgeous and the children are in heaven with it, because they feel they designed it and built it themselves, and are very proud of their own home. They no longer sleep in crowded dormitories, they share rooms with two or three others, no more. Those children feel that we are their guardian angels, because of how much we mind them.

Where we got involved with other orphanages, we just put in systems and procedures, or perhaps a new kitchen. We didn't put ourselves in. We couldn't be everywhere at the one time. There were seventeen orphanages in our area and Derek Tracy and I decided we would go and visit every one of them. Even just by walking through the door, standards would already begin to rise. Once someone takes an interest, the situation improves. Even those institutions that didn't have good practice, once they knew we were coming, the children would be washed and clean, as would rooms, toilets and kitchens. Derek's name preceded him. Orphanage directors were regularly in contact with each other. Because Derek was senior management in the prison system in Ireland, they had huge respect for him. Also, they quickly passed the word around that he was a meticulous observer, one who never missed a trick. Where he found good practice, he was quick to applaud it, which the directors appreciated. Where procedures were less impressive, he was tactful about making recommendations rather than laying down the law. He was the very same with me, always encouraging rather than critical.

I was trained by him to look for signs to tell me if this was really a lovely orphanage, or if it was just lovely for the day. For example, many of the places we went into had playrooms full of toys, which was wonderful, except that the toys had never been out of the presses. You can tell that instantly, from the dust rings for example.

Why does this happen? Sometimes it's just too much trouble for carers to unlock the cupboards and tidy up later. More often, it's because the state makes the carer sign for the toys that are there, a precise inventory, when they start work. At the end of the carer's term there is a further audit and everything has to be there. If it isn't, she will be responsible for the loss of it. The replacement cost may even be taken out of her wages. So it's easier not to let the children near the toys and these playrooms end up looking like your granny's good room, a room that no one ever uses.

Derek, Ger Ashmore and myself, armed with our shiny new clipboards, went around all the orphanages at one stage and decided to try to raise all the ships with the swelling tide. I was getting a lot of publicity out there at the time, so every time I went anywhere there would be a photograph of us

Myself and Igor, rarely apart, and a gang of our children in Margaret Driver's greenhouse.

Little Ivan proudly reading Trish and myself a fairy tale from the Braille book that his teacher had made for him.

Our girls' house – the first pink building in a Russian state orphanage. Every detail was designed by our team of children. A nearly impossible task!

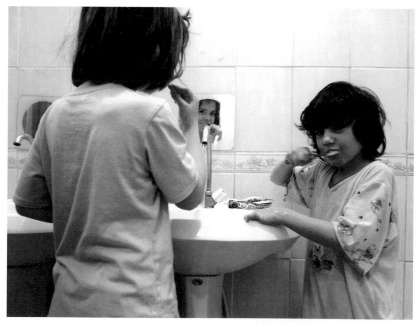

Our little ones getting used to the luxury of their new accommodation before bedtime – toothpaste, toothbrushes and fluffy towels.

The old laundry building in Hortolova (1998).

Our lovely laundry lady waits in anticipation for the new Mieles to arrive.

Zina's class that we found on Day 1 (1998). Now all are successful young adults. This class was the reason we stayed.

Catya and the flower. One of our beautiful children on the Kellogg's programme. She was abandoned aged twelve.

Above: Lena Krychova getting married. Our first wedding. Lena is like one of my own daughters. One of my proudest moments was her wedding.

Left: Evelyn Forde, one of our many wonderful volunteers. Their only agenda was TLC.

One of our beautiful boys, Sergey, leaving us for the army and national service.

Two brothers meeting on one of our sibling trips. They had been separated two years earlier after being taken from their mother.

Trish in usual Trish spirits – I couldn't have done all the travelling without her. Just after this photo was taken she was attacked by a swarm of mosquitoes and took weeks to recover.

Máirtín in 'elf' mode, greeting a little girl who had just arrived into the shelter to which we were bringing some Christmas magic.

Our tenth anniversary gift to the children was the biggest and best party we could manage: bouncy castles, clowns, ice cream and jelly. No orphanage had ever seen anything like it.

Jerome Westbrooks with our children – basketball coach and a hero to them, as well as their first sight of someone with black skin.

Myself, Brendan O'Connor and Marian Keyes, two of the wonderful celebrities who have supported us on the Irish side and generously give their time. Without them we are nothing.

Mikey and his three friends, waxed and frozen, played matches against many boys from our orphanages, loved every moment and learned what a privileged life they have at home.

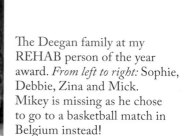

The Deegan family at my REHAB person of the year award. *From left to right:* Sophie, Debbie, Zina and Mick. Mikey is missing as he chose to go to a basketball match in Belgium instead!

Myself and my mammy. She made the transition from Ireland to Russia seamless. She is adored by us all.

in the paper, discussing the improving childcare systems. In fairness, the systems were improving, so I never minded.

At a certain point, the Department of Education in Bryansk decided they were going to stick it to the Irish; that they were going to renovate orphanages to an even better standard than us, which of course we were delighted with. And they did start that process, but large budgets could sometimes dwindle to less than half the amount, because the money just trickled away, often in unclear directions. Little did we know how similar Ireland was!

Derek had a great eye for best practice and his theory was that you didn't need to have money for this. For example, we might go into a place that had no budget for toilet roll and there would be no toilet roll, whereas in another place, also without a budget, the director would have cut up squares of newspaper and stuck them on a piece of string. It cost him nothing to do it but it was good practice. We were naturally always more inclined to support the guy who had the newspaper on the bit of string, because we knew that if we gave him money he would put it to very good use.

An excellent example of this is an orphanage for blind children where we have been involved since 2005. It's a very small, sweet place, in a poor town, but with a fantastic orphanage director and wonderful staff. They appealed to us for help – specifically, they wanted computers with braille keyboards for the children. If anyone appeals to us, we always go and take a look. But we don't work there unless I like and trust the director. Everything hinges on my relationship with him, and I don't mean that in an arrogant way, just that I have to believe that he is doing a good job before I'll commit Irish people's money and myself.

This orphanage is an extraordinary place to visit, very emotional. The children there are partially blind and blind, but there are no white sticks, no dark glasses and no guide dogs. I don't know how they manage; to be an orphan in Russia is incredibly tough, full of endless challenges; the difficulties facing a blind one are almost unimaginable.

The first time we visited, the teachers made a big fuss, as always happens, because we're westerners. I don't like that, I prefer to just sit quietly at a desk in a classroom and let the teacher get on with what they're doing so I can have a good look around. I went into this classroom, said good morning, blabbed away in my bad Russian, and then sat down beside a boy – who was taller than me – at the front desk. I turned round to him and said, 'My name is Debbie, what's your name?' The very first thing he did was to put his hand up and feel my face. Like an idiot, I was totally unprepared for this. The impact was so intimate and strange. I started to cry, the tears just flowed and he started wiping them away. Well, that was the end of that, I was in floods! I apologised, but he didn't seem to mind, he told me not to be sad.

His name was Ivan and he was the same size as my son. If you find yourself connecting with these children on a personal level, because they remind you of someone, you're caught. Ivan had been sent to an institution as a baby, and abandoned completely at the age of four – his parents simply never came back to visit. I was just bowled over by this beautiful boy, who was a very talented musician, and the uncertainty of his future. He was sixteen and due to leave the orphanage, but they were trying to hold on to him because they didn't know where he was going to go.

As it happened, a child in Loughrea tragically died around this time, and his mother contacted us shortly after the funeral. She and her husband wanted to set up a scholarship in their son's name. I chose Ivan to be the recipient, and so one year after I met him, when we were presenting the scholarship, he came to Hortolova with his minder. Now, I hadn't seen him in a full year, but he got out of that car and walked straight over to me and put his arms around me. I hadn't said a single word. He said that he could smell my perfume. I've been wearing the same perfume – Calvin Klein 'Eternity' – for fifteen years; in fact, the little ones in Hortolova spray their teddies with it before I leave following each visit. As he accepted the scholarship, he made a heart-rending speech about how no one had ever given him anything before, or tried to help him in any way.

We moved him out of the orphanage for the blind and to a university that was completely set up for his disability, where he studied music. It cost a couple of grand a year to keep him at this college, and he got through and went on to become a professional musician. He has spread his wings, thanks to the generosity of that family in Loughrea. Russia is a good place to be a musician – there are concerts for everything, all the time – concerts for spring, for summer, for Christmas, for birthdays, feast days, celebrations ... Russians love concerts and parties. If I had a rouble for every concert I've attended, my problems would be over!

We had to try very hard to stay focused on what we were doing, because the hard-luck stories just kept coming. John Mulligan always said, 'Don't look left or right. Just stick to your project. There's always somebody's granny who's in a wheelchair. Stop listening to the stories. You can't fix everyone.' He was ruthless with me. And I suppose he needed to be. I found it very hard to say no to somebody whose nephew needed a wheelchair and who was asking for €200 in the days when we had €200,000 in the bank. But that €200,000 was invariably already stretching so much to cover our projects that I had to learn to be ruthless.

That was, of course, except where it related to our Hortolova children. To them, I have never said no, in fourteen years. They would send letters to the office, looking for help – anything from phone credit, to a heart operation, to finding a mother, or tracing a father in prison. Once I knew it was legitimate, I never said no to a child's request. Some of our staff criticise me for it, but they end up saying, 'There's no point in having a conversation about it, you're going to say yes anyway.'

And we never turn our backs on the children. For as long as they need us, we're there. Even if they end up in prison. And yes, it has happened. But only once. Generally, we are unbelievably successful at keeping them out – when you consider that the national average of orphan boys who go on to prison is thirty-odd per cent, our record is remarkable. These boys tend to go from one institution to another, becoming rougher, more aggressive, more dysfunctional human beings along the way.

There is no safety net to prevent this in Russia. No system to intervene and help these children, stop them becoming the hopeless cases that so many eventually are. And there are odder, more surreal things that happen. I've heard of women put in prison for stealing bread and milk, and staying there for ten years because no one bothers to get them out. Perhaps they break the rules while they're in there, or behave violently, and their sentence gets increased. Perhaps it's simply that no one pays the bribe or agitates for their release. No wonder the population is so terrified of the system and so terrified of breaking laws.

We got a letter one day, to the orphanage, from the mother of a little girl called Natasha. The mother had been locked up ten years previously for stealing and she had written to every single orphanage in the region, trying to find out where her little girl had been sent. It took years for her to track Natasha down because there was no computerised link-up, but finally this letter arrived with us. So of course we contacted the prison and set up a visit with one of our staff, Inna. She went to the prison to meet the mother, with a bag full of chicken and vegetables. And eventually, a year or so later, the mother got out and came to our nearest town and we linked the child with her. They are still in touch. They hadn't seen each other in twelve or fourteen years at that stage, and in Russia there is no facility for supporting such reconnections with any psychological back-up or assistance. The state simply doesn't do that, although they are conscious they need to and are working on it. In the absence of trained help, how do two people begin to forge a relationship? Or heal a child's wounds?

Psychologists call it an attachment wound, and it's like a big, black gaping hole at the centre of a child's being. It's a wound they will try to fill with anything – stealing, telling lies, bullying, forcing people to hate them. Low self-esteem is a classic symptom, as is addiction in later life. Some children suffer more than others, some don't manifest it until they are adults. But every one of our children was suffering to some degree from an attachment wound and our mission was to help them overcome it, to heal it with the first unconditional love most of them had ever known.

9

THE ONES WE COULDN'T SAVE

We have buried four children during the years of To Russia With Love, and every one of us lost a piece of our heart on those days. In my opinion, there is nothing sadder than an orphan's funeral.

The first tragedy was another orphan girl called Natasha, who was thirteen when she died. She was a gentle beauty and cared for her younger brother. She wasn't a particularly wayward child, but she got out of the orphanage one night and met up with three family children from the local village. It was a freezing cold night, maybe minus 30°C, and the four of them got into a car in a garage and turned on the ignition, to keep warm. The next day the four bodies were found; they had poisoned themselves by accident. Without To Russia With Love, Natasha's grave wouldn't have had a headstone or been covered with flowers. There was no one else there.

Then there was a little boy, Sergei, who was ten. He went home for a weekend, which very few of them ever do, because their parents are so dysfunctional that they don't have homes, or aren't fit to mind their children even for a couple of days. Sergei's mum was an alcoholic, but he was desperate to get back to her all the time. He was terribly attached and miserable without her. So he went home, and the mother was drinking and smoking the first night he got there and passed out with a lit cigarette in her hand. The mattress went on fire, but she couldn't move because she was so drunk. The next day they found Sergei wrapped around her body. He must have been trying to wake her up, or protect her from the flames and then passed out from the smoke. Again we arranged the funeral and the Irish flowers were the only flowers on the grave.

About three years into To Russia With Love, I was at the orphanage one day and these two little twins arrived, a boy, Micha, and a girl, Ustya, about ten years old. Her hair had been shaved, because in Russia they don't have head lice cream so they just whip off the hair if there are lice. She was tiny and obviously had special needs, and he was clearly her minder and protector, although he was so tiny himself. They were two very small, weak children, with their little old leather suitcases. If you happen to be there on a day when children first arrive, you tend to connect with them specially. Dermot Hearne, a deeply caring man, a trainer from Wheatfield Prison, was there with me on this particular day, overseeing the building of a lovely playground designed by the prisoners in Dublin. So we sat down with these two and were trying to comfort them. Ustya was wearing an old-fashioned, pink knitted dress and because of nerves was pulling at a loose strand. Dermot was terrified the whole thing was going to unravel and was doing his best to save it. Micha had learned a sailor dance in the previous orphanage, so he was doing his little dance, trying to cheer her up.

About three years after they arrived, Micha was out on the train tracks one day – there are train tracks everywhere in the Russian countryside. Normally they are reasonably safe, but somehow Micha was electrocuted. He must have got hold of a wire, or something. I was in Connemara on holidays when it happened; Igor called me to say Micha was in hospital and the doctors thought he would die that night because he had third degree burns over ninety per cent of his little body. He was thirteen at the time.

I felt I knew Micha particularly well, so my instant reaction was, 'I need to go there, now.' I knew the hospital situation as well and I knew the kind of care an orphan child could expect. So I got to Dublin in the early hours, got the flight to Moscow, then the train and arrived at the hospital within about twenty-four hours. It was midnight. I went straight to the burns unit – I don't know why they call it that, because nothing is different, it's just like any other ward – and I nearly passed out. Between organising my various tickets and my journey, I hadn't thought or prepared properly for what was ahead. Igor had tried to put me off, but I ignored his advice.

Micha was in an old hospital bed and he was completely black, burned to a crisp. From his mouth down, he was charred, like a burned pizza. From his mouth up, he was absolutely perfect. I have no idea why, but there was this clear dividing line halfway across his face. To stop him tearing at himself, they had tied his hands to the top of the bed and his legs to the bottom, with rags. They hadn't given him morphine, so he was in terrible, terrible pain. When I saw him, my first action was to run outside and vomit, then I pulled myself together and went back in, sat beside him and smiled as I fixed his blond hair.

He should have been dead already by the time I arrived, but he continued to live. I sat beside his bed for six days and six nights. I told him stories, talked to him and cried. He came in and out of consciousness, though mostly the pain was too bad for him to bear. On my last day he said, 'I'm sorry if I was bold. Can you please mind Ustya for me?' I promised him that I would. Eventually I had to leave, I couldn't stay any more, we had no idea how much longer he would last. I had to go home. I got the train to Moscow. It was Mother's Day I remember and I was conscious of getting home to see my three children.

Micha died about twenty minutes after I left, but my staff didn't tell me until the next day. My children were giving me their Mother's Day cards and all I could think of was this poor child and the agony he suffered, and where was his mother.

The period following Micha's death is the only time I ever agreed to go into therapy. My board insisted. I couldn't cook anything for months, could barely eat, because I had the smell constantly in my nostrils, that awful smell of charred flesh. I did do the therapy, because they insisted, but I didn't find it much use. The therapist told me I had no boundaries and I needed to work on that. But I never did. I have amazing friends and I off-load all the trauma on them. I talk it out.

At Micha's funeral, there was no one except Marion Kilbride, a director of the charity and minder of many, Ustya, and a handful of our children and Russian staff. We paid for the coffin, the grave and the flowers. In Russia, orphans go into a paupers' grave. Ustya is nineteen now and is still under our wing, because I promised Micha and because she still needs us. We gave her a little extra, because she lost him and he was her only protector.

The most heart-breaking of our losses – because he was twenty and we had all known him since he was seven years old – came two years ago and was a boy called Kolya. He was probably the brightest and most bubbly child in the orphanage, with the most beautiful smile. He was good-looking, charming and intelligent, and very close to us from a young age. He loved the Irish. Máirtín taught him how to play the guitar. Not all of the children bonded equally; some were more reserved, less trusting. Over time, they all fell in love with us, but initially some were more hostile. Kolya was not one of these. He was ours from day one.

We knew Kolya had an older brother somewhere, but we didn't know where, we couldn't trace him. It took us years to trace the siblings of our orphans – it's very difficult in Russia, because there's no paper trail once they leave the institutions. If they run away – and a lot of them run away, even though there's not much out there for them except sex trafficking and crime – unless the police catch them and bring them back, there's no further effort made to trace them or find out what happened to them. So Kolya was alone in the world, as far as we knew, but was dearly loved by carers and children alike at the orphanage for his smiley, sweet-natured temperament.

At the time he was twenty and living in accommodation paid for and managed by us in the local town. It's something we have been doing for the children who leave the orphanage once they get too old. It is very expensive, we simply can't sustain it any more unless we get more donors, but while they are there, we know they're safe. All our boys have to go into the army for their military service, and usually when they come out, they don't speak for weeks. They are slightly shell-shocked, due to the harshness of the regime. We have to nurture them back to being human again.

If you go to college, you can put off going into the army, but for those who don't, they go straight from the orphanage. Some of them want to go – they like the institutional life, but invariably when they come back, they are vacant. There are millions of soldiers in Russia, they are everywhere. In the train stations at night, you can see thousands of young men getting onto these 1 kilometre-long trains – all trains in Russia are exactly 1 kilometre long – with newly shaved heads, the tramp-tramp of their boots and the snow falling as they say goodbye to loved ones. It's like something out of an old black-and-white movie. But what's waiting for the new young recruits is usually incredibly harsh. It's physically gruelling and there are huge bullying problems, from the top down, which naturally get more severe and savage as they move down through the ranks to these eighteen-year-old children.

We mind their few belongings while they're gone – a ring maybe, the precious suitcase. We supply them with a mobile phone and credit as much as we can, and we do our best to keep in contact with them. It's nearly impossible, because they are moved around. But at least once they get out, they have somewhere to go. They know where to find us and once we get them back, we nurse them, we try and set them up again in life, help them get jobs.

Kolya didn't make it to the army.

It was November 2011 and I had just arrived in Moscow with Joanna Fortune, our manager, and Catrina Sheridan, a board member and long-standing mentor to me. We were on our way to the orphanage when I got the call. Kolya was dead. We were told that he had committed suicide. He had supposedly thrown himself under a train and was decapitated. Except that we all knew he couldn't have, that he wouldn't have done that.

Kolya was doing extremely well in life. He was on our Leaver's Programme, was in college, and an incredibly personable young man, well liked by everybody who met him. His sponsor, John Patchell, had just arrived in Moscow with his family for a short break and Kolya was due to meet up with him the next day. He was counting down the hours to seeing John. It just didn't make sense.

I got to our flat in Bryansk and children started arriving from everywhere. We have created an incredible family of children over the years. There are hundreds of them, in touch via Facebook, every day, with each other. And bit by bit they began pouring into the flat. Children we hadn't seen in years, who had grown up and gone out into the world, started knocking on the door. Word got out and all night they came. Our flat has become a family home for those who have left, the place they all come back to when something happens. The kettle went on many times. Olga Stepanova, our darling head minder and mama to many, cooked, shopped and wept with me as we tried to cope with the numbers of children arriving. The children found a picture of Kolya and put it in a frame on the table and lit a candle in front of it. Our beautiful big boys, his classmates, took over. They went to identify what was left of him and choose a suit for his very broken body. The children chose the coffin, the flowers and the gravesite. They wrote prayers and words about their friend.

Gradually the story, such as it was, began coming out. The bigger boys were hearing snippets of information from various sources.

It appeared that Kolya owed money, $400, to a criminal and couldn't pay. So two or three local thugs had poured vodka into him, forced him to drink a bottle or whatever of the stuff, and then laid him unconscious on the tracks when the train was coming. The police were keen to put it down to suicide, because if it was suspected murder, they would have had to investigate and, after all, he was only an orphan, so what was the point? It would have been, to their mind, a waste of paperwork. At the autopsy, Kolya was found to be well over the legal alcohol limit and a bottle of vodka had been found by the body, although his friends all knew he never drank vodka. He hated it.

We went to the morgue to collect the body, a big gang of us

together. In Russia they have a morgue for normal citizens and one for criminals. Kolya was considered a criminal because he had apparently committed suicide, so that was the morgue he was assigned to. In all my years in Russia, I have never seen anything like this. We went down a pot-holed, overgrown lane, to a massive warehouse. John Patchell, who had been in Moscow waiting for Kolya, came down to meet us and support me. The mortician came out to us. He was wearing a white apron, like a butcher's apron, and he was just dripping in blood. He had on rubber gloves, also dripping with blood. It was like something you'd see in a Frankenstein movie. Behind him was a huge room, like an abattoir, and all I could see were ancient trollies, left over from some war by the look of them, with bodies on them. You could see legs, arms, heads, sticking out and blood everywhere. I think I will take the image of that mortuary to my grave. They don't seem to have the same decorum around death in Russia as I'm used to in Ireland, but possibly that's because I've only attended orphans' funerals there, where there are no frills or flowers.

The mortician asked if we wanted to come in. John Patchell said yes. I couldn't. They somehow pieced Kolya together and brought him out to us. There was cloth over parts of the body, and they had put some kind of a shroud over him, to physically hold him together, and they brought him out and put him in the coffin we had bought for him. Our orphan boys helped

145

dress him in the suit they had chosen for him. The situation was so undignified. I had somehow assumed that a chauffeur-driven limo would arrive to take him and us to the grave, as it would in Ireland. Instead, we all got on this rattly old bus, they opened the back, like a luggage door, and slid the coffin down the centre between our seats. The children sat quietly with their hands on the lid of the coffin as the bus trundled towards our small country graveyard. I wasn't prepared for any of it, for the sheer indignity and overwhelming sadness.

We couldn't bring Kolya to a church, because he was said to have committed suicide and so the priest wouldn't bury him. Christian my ass! Russia today is like Ireland was thirty years ago, no suicides on consecrated grounds. The children were really upset, because they wanted his body to go to God, but there was nothing we could do, except conduct the service ourselves, which we did. The children dug the hole, taking it in turns with their shovels. They put the box in the grave, filled it in and then began what is a tradition around death in Russia. They put a tablecloth on the mound of raw earth and there's food and everybody drinks and eats around the grave. It's a cultural thing, to celebrate the passing over. The children had bought huge wreaths, the way they do in Russia, and they put one on the grave from me, as his mother. When I saw that, it finished me. I was so glad to have Noel Quinn, friend to me and the children, and John Patchell with me at the grave.

We all began to say a few words about Kolya, as well as any of us was able. I can't tell you how upsetting it was to have no family there, no one except other orphan children and charity workers, to say goodbye to a wonderful young man, someone we had known since he was a delightful child.

Kolya's story ended there, although we did find a priest, a decent, compassionate man, to say mass for him after forty days. In Russia there is always a mass forty days after someone dies – it's like our month's mind. One of our amazing people on the ground found this priest and told him the whole story about Kolya and about our suspicions. At the same time, a social worker from Kolya's college was determined to find out the truth and fought tooth and nail to get the full story. The police eventually gave in and said there was enough evidence to suggest it hadn't been suicide, although they weren't going to consider it murder either. I think death by misadventure was the official line. But it was enough to have a proper mass said for him after forty days, and the children went and felt better for it. Pain is very much part of their lives over there.

We did contemplate paying a lawyer to chase down the full story, to make it all right, but it would have cost upwards of €5,000 and in the end, we decided we would be better off spending it on the living rather than the dead. All the people who mattered knew that Kolya didn't commit suicide, that he was murdered by a bunch of people who knew, because he was an orphan, no one would really care.

We miss him every day. We have been to his grave in deep snow and in summer heat. Máirtín has played his guitar there for him, in case he's listening. We have brought his Santa presents and laid them there for him. The children have built a picket fence and have planted flowers, which now grow over his grave.

10

JOE DUFFY, BARRETSTOWN AND BESLAN

The Beslan tragedy in numbers:

Total numbers of hostages: 1,100

Number of people killed: 334

> *Children aged 1–17 years: 186*
>
> *Teachers/school staff: 17*
>
> *Fighters of special troops of FSB: 10*
>
> *Staff of the Ministry of Emergency Situations: 2*
>
> *Relatives, guests and friends of pupils: 118*
>
> *Militiamen: 1*

66 families lost from 2 to 6 people, and 17 children became orphans

There are no official figures for the relatives of victims who have subsequently died as a result of psychological trauma.

I was at home watching TV with my family one evening, when suddenly these unbelievable images came on the news of a school hall in Russia packed with children, parents and terrorists. Over 1,000 people were taken hostage, including children as young as one year old. Three hundred and thirty-four were killed during a hideous, brutal three-day siege that ultimately achieved nothing. Most of those killed were children. I'd never heard of Beslan – it's 4,000 to 5,000 kilometres from where we are in Russia; a small town, a village really, in North Ossetia – but I, along with the rest of this country, was riveted by the horror that unfolded there.

A gang of Chechen separatists, including female fighters who were dubbed the Black Widows, moved into the school at First Bell, 1 September. This is the day the little junior infants start school for the first time and it's a really big deal in Russia. Parents go with their children to help settle them in, they bring cameras and take photos and film clips. It's normally a proud, happy time. So all the mums had arrived and some dads too. A van pulled up behind them, out came the militants, locked all the school doors and kept them in there for three days. They gave them no food, no water, no medicine. They weren't allowed use the toilets or even open the windows. They were kept in this sweltering, stinking gym. Some mothers were sent out with their smallest children and forced to leave the older ones behind. The fathers were made to strap bombs to basketball nets hanging from each end of the hall. In some cases they had to strap the wires of the bombs to children's legs. If they moved, the bomb would detonate. The teachers and parents stripped the children of their clothes to try to keep them cool. Some of them were given their own urine to drink to keep them hydrated. The cruellest of the militants were apparently the women, the Black Widows. They had lost husbands and children themselves, yet – or perhaps because of this – they showed no mercy or pity for the children of others.

The militants were looking for an end to the Second Chechen War and Russian withdrawal from Chechnya. There were attempts at negotiation, but nothing successful and, after three days of stand-off, the Russian military stormed the building, in their usual heavy-handed way, with tanks and rockets. There was a bloodbath. Nearly 200 children were killed over the three days.

It was horrific to watch – children's dead bodies being carried out of the rubble of the school, children with terrible wounds, starving, dehydrated and traumatised. Families searching for missing loved ones, fathers reading through the list of dead, looking for the names of their wives and children. The pain of it all hit Irish people very hard. Broadcaster Joe Duffy is a neighbour of mine and he was deeply disturbed by it. He talked about it on *Liveline* and discovered that half the country felt the same way. There was a national desire to reach out, to help in some way, so Joe suggested opening an account, where people could donate money if they wished, and said, 'Debbie Deegan is a neighbour of mine – she has an office in Clontarf, why don't we let her administer the money?'

I didn't know how much money would come in, or what we would do with it. Was it for the families? The tragedy? The therapy? Money was never going to make the situation better for the people of Beslan, but our instant reaction here, in the face of an atrocity or a natural disaster, is to gather money and send it. It's a kind and good impulse.

So we opened an account. I was nervous about doing it, because I didn't know Beslan and our mission statement only covers us to work with orphans. But we made a decision in the office that we would help. In the first three months €600,000 came in; one young man from Kerry cycled from Moscow to Ireland to raise money. People actually queued outside our office in Clontarf to donate and to sign a condolence book. Actually, there were condolence books being prepared all over the country, by schools, towns, old folk's homes. A school of small, deaf boys came to Orwell Road, to the Russian Embassy itself, and wanted to formally offer their condolences. The embassy hadn't thought to set anything up, because they really hadn't expected this, but they got a table and chair and a book, and thousands of people began to sign it. The ambassador – a wonderful man called Vladimir Rakmanin – and the embassy staff were all unbelievably moved by the outpouring of goodwill. Eventually the condolence book was moved to the Mansion House, to cope with the huge numbers.

Trish and I decided to go to Beslan and see what was needed, and take some of these books with us, just a selection of the most beautiful ones. We had no intention of taking the money until we saw where it could best be spent. The Irish embassy in Moscow (the ambassador at the time was Justin Harman) warned us not to go, because the authorities feared that the men of Beslan would retaliate against the Ingush and Chechens once the initial mourning period was over. They expected huge problems. Chechnya is just over the border from Beslan, it's about the same distance as Dalkey to Clontarf, and is a very troubled region. Igor didn't want me to go either and initially said he wouldn't come with me, but once he saw that I was determined, he of course came along. Meanwhile, a beautiful young woman called Oksana, who lived in County Cavan, contacted us after hearing the story on Joe Duffy's show, to say that her family lived in Beslan and she would come with us to show us the ropes. We were delighted to have a personal connection, as in Russia personal connections are everything. All the same, to say we hadn't a clue what was ahead of us is putting it mildly.

We packed backpacks with these beautiful condolence

books, because we didn't want to let them go through customs, and at this stage Adrian McCarthy, the filmmaker who had made the documentary about Zina for TV3, came on board. He had decided there was a story there, so he simply knocked on the door and asked to follow us. He got funding from RTÉ and made *The Journey of the Books* out of the trip.

It was forty days after the tragedy by the time we got to Beslan, a very holy day. The whole town had been praying and the mourning period was up now, and no one knew quite what would happen, whether there would be retaliations. We flew into the tiny airport outside Vladikavkaz, over magnificent snow-covered mountains. The graveyard is about two minutes' drive away, so the first thing we did was stop there. It was maybe seven in the evening, just getting dim, and it was autumn, so the colours were magnificent. The graveyard was completely surrounded by huge trees, with thousands of crows sitting in them, all cawing loudly.

There were hundreds of new graves there; most belonged to children. The earth was raw and churned-looking. Some family plots had several fresh mounds, where three or four children from the same family, or a mother and two children, had been killed. The babushkas were lying on the dirt, wailing and tearing at their clothes. My memory of that evening is like a scene from a nightmare; the women howling and the crows cawing. It was eerie and awful. We took some of the books out of our bags and put them on the graves. A pointless gesture perhaps, but what else can you do in the face of such tragedy?

We stayed the night in an old sanatorium out in the forest, because the hotels were not considered safe. We were locked into our rooms. The next day we went to meet the mayor and that was total chaos. Camera crews from all over the world were in Beslan, waiting to see what would happen next. Queuing behind us were Danish, Italians, Australians, all with donations that they were simply handing over. I wonder does anyone know where that money ended up? Serious amounts of cash, accompanied by goodwill alone, will never reach their intended destination.

We sat in on a committee meeting at the town hall where the women were shrieking because they were getting no answers. And they were screaming at each other. Women who had lost children were turning on those who hadn't, especially where the other woman had been in the school and had got out with her own children. 'Why did she not help get my children out?' they were shouting, deranged with grief and bitterness. They turned on the school principal, a seventy-year-old woman, and accused her of being involved, of having let the separatists in over the summer to lay bombs under the school floorboards, so that by the time they arrived the bombs were already in situ, making their task much easier. It's a theory that has since been officially denied, but Russia has a blame culture, there always has to be a culprit, and so they turned on this woman and screamed accusations at her.

The day after this, we went to the school itself. We probably shouldn't have been allowed, in that it should still have been a crime scene, but that wasn't the case. There was no yellow tape and definitely no Horatio Caine from *CSI*. Just a shattered school. As we walked up to it, we saw thousands of plastic bottles of water lining the way, literally thousands. The mothers had left them there. The children had been severely dehydrated, not allowed food or water over three days in intense heat, because it was a particularly hot autumn. Some died of dehydration in the gym and others were so weak that they couldn't escape when the fire broke out and the Russian army stormed the place. So the mums came afterwards, with water, because their babies had died for lack of it.

We went into the gymnasium of this rundown, old-fashioned school. Every one of us was silenced at the impact of walking onto what had seemed like a film set on the news but was now reality; the place where we had watched such tragedy unfold a month earlier. The walls were covered in dried blood. There were little shoes and shredded clothing lying around. As we walked in, we were told that the body of a mother was being taken down from the room beside us. She had prayed for forty days, then, unable to cope with the pain, hanged herself.

She wasn't the only one; many others hanged themselves in that school in the weeks after the tragedy, or so we were told. Information was unreliable though, as chaos ruled.

There was a woman sitting on the floor as we entered the school hall. She called me over to show me a plastic lunch box and told me, 'We can't find my son. I know he must have run away. I bring his lunch every day because I know he's going to come back.' She was frantic, showing photos of the boy and telling me this story, determined to believe her son was still alive. So many of the hostages were blown literally to bits during the storming of the building that there was no DNA evidence – forensics weren't that sophisticated there; children were still missing, but no one could tell their mothers what had happened to them. This woman was showing me all the food she had packed in the lunch box, waiting for her son to come back.

We walked through corridors that had literally thousands of bullet holes. One of the cooks took us down to the kitchen and showed us these big pots with lids on them, where they had hidden some of the smallest junior infants. Those children were saved. There were classrooms full of blood, shredded copybooks and torn clothing. At First Bell, the girls all appear with their hair done up in beautiful, traditional ribbons. Blood-soaked remnants of these were everywhere. Our camera crew and interpreter were wiping away endless tears. None of us knew what to say. There's no speaking in some situations. We went in, in good faith, with these beautiful condolence books, but once there we just did not know how to express our sympathy in any way that would count. Joe Duffy interviewed me for *Liveline* from Beslan. That was one of the hardest interviews I've ever done, trying to describe the horrors that we saw.

Certainly money was never going to solve these people's problems. President Vladimir Putin had said they were going to rebuild, that they would create the best school in Russia, and Russia is a rich country, it has funds to do this, so they didn't actually need money for this particular project. They needed so much, but not that. However, money was what we had – this fund donated by the people of Ireland, an expression of their solidarity and sympathy. And so we had to spend it. We wanted a substantial project, something specific, rather than just handing over cash.

We came home and this pot of money was keeping me awake at night. What to do with it? We decided to send in psychologists, who were so clearly needed, but there was no point sending Irish psychologists. They would have had no understanding of the Russian psyche and anyway would have had to work through an interpreter, which would have meant they lost 50 per cent of their value. We needed a Russian solution to this Russian problem, not an idealistic Irish one.

So we went to Moscow and found an incredible organisation called Broken Flower that had been set up for traumatised children about ten years previously, when a tower block in Moscow was blown up. Broken Flower worked with the survivors and had wonderful psychologists. We paid them for two years to go to Beslan on a regular basis. They did drawing, jigsaw therapy, sand and art therapy with the children, spoke to them and helped them begin to come to terms with their loss and trauma. Peter Hanlon, a great friend of mine and one of the best grief therapists in Ireland, monitored the project on our behalf.

We also sat down with the people behind Barretstown – an excellent organisation – in Ireland. They normally work with children with cancer, but they agreed to help with our project. At that stage we had met many of the families in Beslan and had become friendly with some of them. We wanted to take them away from the scene of their heartbreak, at least physically, for a time. They needed to be taken out of that tragic town.

We chartered a plane and flew 100 of the wounded children and their parents to Barretstown for rest and recuperation. And it was the best thing we could have done. The children arrived into this beautiful big old Irish castle – built in the sixteenth century, it was Elizabeth Arden's country home in 1962 – which had play rooms, therapy rooms, drawing rooms, fun everywhere. Many of them were accompanied by their fathers, who were the ones left behind. It was the mothers who had gone with the children on the first day and been killed – so these fathers came with their children. Big, heavy Russian men, with bottles of vodka in their suitcases and packets of cigarettes in their pockets. Now, in Barretstown, drinking and smoking are totally prohibited; the kids who are normally there have cancer, so there is absolutely no smoking, not even any smoking areas. It's just not allowed.

The first night they all arrived, I got a phone call: 'Debbie, you need to come down here, they're all smoking and drinking.' So I went down and spoke to the fathers. These men were severely grieving. They practically didn't know where they were – they'd landed in this castle in the middle of Kildare and everyone was throwing money and kindness at them. We couldn't do enough for them – magicians, new clothes, the circus, trips to Powerscourt. It was do-lally land … these men were still totally lost, blitzed by what had happened to them. They just weren't able for it all. So I went to the management and grief therapists in Barretstown, who were fantastic, and said, 'These men have bigger issues than you telling them to stop smoking …' Their response was amazing. The camp was closed to everyone else for the three weeks, but cigarette smoke does linger, so a separate cottage was allocated to these Russian fathers, so they could drink when they needed to and smoke all day, which was their norm. These were unique guests so unique rules had to be drawn up.

The children, as well as being wounded, had almost all lost a loved one – a sibling, sometimes two, often a mother as well. We spent three weeks with them, offering every kind of fun activity you can imagine, as well as therapy and bereavement counselling if they wanted it. In Russia, no one makes an obvious show of their emotions. They think we're mad the way we show our feelings.

At the end of the three weeks, we had a reception in Clontarf Castle for the families, and Joe Duffy came and made a beautiful speech. The daddies broke down, these big, hard Russian men. They couldn't believe how much the Irish had done for them. For many, it was the first time they had any respite, or kindness, or space since the tragedy. Some of them still write to me, six years later. We may have thought that turning up with our condolence books and donating funds was a useless response to such overwhelming tragedy, but there were many people who drew huge solace from the support, and connections were made that lasted well beyond the initial outpouring of shock and sympathy.

Ireland may be a tiny country, but Irish warmth spreads far and with huge effect.

After I appeared on Andrei Malakhov's TV show last year (of which more later), a woman emailed me. She was one of the few mothers who were on the trip to Barretstown, and her memories of the warmth and kindness of people in Ireland still lights up her life now.

Reproduction of an email from Larissa Azieva, sent January 2011:

Dear Debby,

May be you remember me. I am Larissa Azieva, an English teacher of school, Beslan, Russia. You've invited us to Ireland in 2005. This evening my daughter rushed into my room and cried: 'Mum, switch the TV on! There's Debby Digan there, that Debby from Ireland!' I enjoyed watching you and your family – your husband, your son, your daughter and your daughter Zina from Russia. You look so wonderful as always! You haven't changed at all. Debby, you're a great woman with a great heart! We remember every minute of our stay in Ireland. It was you who returned our children back to life. You organised our stay so perfectly that the children had forgotten all that horror which they had seen in the gym. It's a pity Andrey Malakhov didn't know about that part of your work. If only I was there at the show I'd tell all Russia about your contribution to cure injured hearts of Beslan's children. THANK YOU VERY MUCH!!!

We love you! We remember you! We'll never forget you and the kindness of the beautiful Irish people.

11

ADOPTIONS AND
THE FACEBOOK ERA

To Russia With Love, as a charitable organisation, does not do adoptions. I personally have assisted couples for years when they have run into trouble or needed advice, either in Ireland or Russia. I have done this on my own time and have never received any type of payment. I have done it because I felt sorry for the couples, who were usually at the end of their tether by the time they got to me. Recently, however, I was told by the International Adoption Agency to desist or there would be consequences. I've never been one to worry about consequences. Generally though, my interest is with the ones who are left behind and not those lucky enough to find homes with families across the world. The children I feel responsible for are those left waving goodbye at the gate, then turning around and going back to their difficult, sad lives.

When Russia began a system of fostering, maybe ten years ago, we were ranting to anyone who would listen about quality and not quantity fostering. The government was giving around $300 a month, which was huge money, to anyone who would foster an orphan, and so people were coming in from villages to take a child or two. Often these foster parents were far from ideal, or just wanted cheap labour. It was a disaster in a lot of cases, half of those we were sending out were coming back, because the children are not always easy to deal with. Their foster parents were expecting grateful, well-behaved, academically normal children. This was never going to be the case. The return to the orphanage felt like a double rejection for those who were sent back.

In fairness, President Putin has made great improvements in the foster care system and these days it works better, but it is still far from perfect. Moreover, I am highly aware that in Ireland the fostering system was also initially far from perfect; children were taken into families where they were expected to provide unpaid labour and often were mistreated. We are rightly ashamed of the way we raised children in Irish institutions and we certainly are not in any position to pontificate about standards and best practice elsewhere. Putin has also slowed down foreign adoption recently, for a variety of reasons, and currently Irish couples cannot adopt from Russia because there is no bilateral agreement between the two countries and Russia is not a member of the Hague Convention. However, if there was a willingness and enthusiasm here, I believe the difficulties of a bilateral agreement could be ironed out.

Adoption can be problematic – although in fairness, we usually only get to hear of the cases where something goes wrong. Many adoptions run smoothly, but some do break down, all over the world. Where the adopted child is taken to a new country, with a new language and customs, obviously the adjustment is harder. For example, over 45,000 Russian children have been officially adopted into American families in the last twenty years, many of them aged five and upwards; these are normally the ones who get left behind, so choosing them is a kind impulse. In my experience American families are also the only ones to actively seek out physically disabled children to adopt, something that I have the height of respect for. But there is also a tradition in America of adoptive parents breaking all ties with a child's background and birth family. They give them new names, new identities and expect them to turn into all-American children overnight, as if they had no past, no family, no years of trauma behind them. They are so keen to provide this child with a new life, that they neglect to value the old one.

American families want a clean slate, a shiny new page, but it doesn't always work like that. This is one reason so many adoptions fail. And now that we live in an era of Facebook, it is easier for these children to contact us and try to revive something of their early lives. These days we frequently get requests out of the blue from children in America, saying, 'Do you remember me?' and asking us to help trace their families.

A year ago, I got a message through Facebook from a girl who said, 'My name is Sandra, I don't know if you remember me ...?' I figured out it was a girl I had known as Sasha, who was adopted with her brother, Uri, many years ago. They were two gorgeous children, Sasha was the elder of the two, and I still have a whole load of photographs of them both. The siblings were adopted together by a well-off American family when they were about five and nine. We said goodbye to them and thought everything was going to be lovely, because they seemed to be going to a kind family. However, within about a year the family situation became very dysfunctional. They lived in a typical American family home – I've seen their prom photos, which were beautiful – but they have been very unhappy.

By the time Sasha, now Sandra, contacted me, she hadn't really been talking to her adopted mum for years, even though she and Uri were both still living at home. Now they desperately wanted to find their grandmother in Russia, who had cared for them as babies, and they also thought they had other siblings. So I went back over their case studies, I found that there were indeed siblings and that the grandmother had been minding them before they came to the orphanage.

I sent a scout, via Igor, to find this grandmother. We went

to her house – she's eighty-three now and blind for the last few years. Her daughter had been an alcoholic, so Granny had taken her four children, but she couldn't mind them all. She was already old by then and going blind, so she kept two and gave the two smallest away in the hopes that they would be adopted. Granny never recovered from giving them away and wrote to them numerous times in America telling them she loved them, but the new mother never passed on her letters.

In fairness, it does happen that the blood relatives of adopted children sometimes come looking for money if they have contact with the new family, but this eighty-three-year-old granny was not one of those. She broke down when we told her why we were calling. She couldn't believe the two children were alive and well, and that she might get to meet them again. We also found their two older sisters and even their mother, who is now a recovered alcoholic. She wrote a shockingly sad letter to the two in America recently, about how she was such a bad mother, how she'd given them away and neglected them. I read it, because we had to translate it, and I could feel her pain. Yes, she gave them away and was a terrible mother, but clearly she didn't stop loving them.

Sasha and Uri want to go and visit, so I am currently making arrangements. We're hoping they will be able to travel over this summer and that Granny will live long enough to be reunited with them.

Sometimes it's the adoptive parents I feel for. I have a pen pal, Malcolm, who emails me regularly from America. I am one of the many women who love him, to whom he tells some of the unbelievable stories about his adopted children. I first saw Malcolm in the orphanage twelve or so years ago, and he had his arm around one of the boys, which made me think, 'Who the hell is he?' I don't like strange men in our orphanage. So I went over to investigate. He turned out to be a tall, decent, well-heeled American man, who had decided to adopt two children and try to give them a better life.

He took in two boys and his life has been challenging, to say the least, since – a catalogue of considerable difficulties. The boys are eighteen and thirteen now, and do have some wonderful traits. The older one seems to be getting on his feet, but the thirteen-year-old is still pressing Malcolm's buttons so hard that any other person would have broken and put him into foster care by now. But Malcolm keeps going. He is one of the best fathers I have ever met. He has a brilliant mind and writes to me regularly about his woes; sometimes hysterically funny, sometimes tragically sad. He has had every parenting challenge thrown at him, from police on his doorstep, to expulsions from school. Sometimes he'll get a nice comment from these boys – 'You're the only person who has ever stood by me.' Such comments are so rare that when they do come he is elated. These children have been rejected by the most important person in their world

– their mother – so for the rest of their lives, many try to repeat the pattern of rejection by pushing away those who try to love them; it's a reaction to trauma and Malcolm knows this. He went into the situation with open eyes and never expected it would be easy. Even though it has been much harder than he could have imagined, if anyone can make it work, Malcolm can.

In the many cases where the adoptions do work out, fate can play a very cruel trick by dividing siblings deeply – giving one a life of wealth and ease, while another continues to struggle daily with the harsh realities of life in Russia. One of my favourite children, Kirill, has just such a story. He was always deep and dark, a difficult child, who hated the Russian system. His mother abandoned him along with his little brother, and every year the mother wrote to the orphanage to say, 'I'm coming back this May to collect you.' Every year he waited, standing at the gate of that orphanage for days, but his mother never arrived. His brother, Alex, a year younger, was an easy child, very unlike Kirill, and was adopted by an American family, who cut off all contact with his old life. Over the years, Kirill became darker, more anti-establishment. He was a child who never smiled. The orphanage staff had problems with him and told him he was never going to amount to much, so he started to believe it. I did think at one stage that we were never going to rescue him, that he would end up in prison, because he had such a bad temper. But he thawed, finally.

Kirill is twenty-four now, an incredible young man and a very gifted carpenter. Despite his lack of education he speaks fluent English. One of the few things he ever did for anyone was to make me the most magnificent bed for the flat in Bryansk. He wanted to do something for me after he left the orphanage and so hand-carved this absolutely beautiful bed. It is my treasured possession, a million euro wouldn't have meant as much to me. I would hope to hand it on to my children and grandchildren one day.

Anyway, two years ago, Kirill asked me if I could find his brother. So I set out to trace this boy, Alex. And it was hard, because in Russia you aren't entitled or encouraged to trace siblings, or even birth parents. But eventually, on Facebook, I located a photograph of this young Adonis, lying on the deck of a yacht in a fancy yacht club; Kirill's identical twin in looks, now called Andy. He seems to have had the perfect American adoption experience. He lives in luxury with devoted parents and great prospects in life. So I emailed the yacht club and asked could I contact the mother? She replied eventually and I asked her could Kirill contact his brother? Initially she was reluctant as she felt it would only upset Andy; he was going to be a lawyer, was a very talented musician, and she didn't want complications in his life. I was mightily offended of course – I said Kirill was a great boy, that he played the accordion and I could only see the benefits of a reunion … We were like two mothers at an Irish dancing competition!

She heard me out, changed her mind and kindly invited Kirill to come and stay. I said no, because it would have been too much for him. This family live in a *Home Alone*-type house in leafy suburban America; Kirill lives in one room of a hostel in the worst part of a Russian mining town. So then, after much to-ing and fro-ing, Andy's mother suggested we allow the boys to swap text messages. To Russia With Love bought Kirill a phone and credit every week, and the two boys started texting. It's the wrong way for brothers to be reunited but it was the best we could do.

They established contact and were in touch fairly regularly, but it all broke down when Andy asked Kirill what he got for Christmas. Kirill doesn't usually get Christmas presents, unless he is visiting at our house in Clontarf, as sometimes happens, and Andy had been given a new red sports car, with a big red ribbon on it. Seriously. He texted a photo of it to Kirill, who was so hurt at the insensitivity, that he ceased all communication. Andy has emailed him since, saying he really misses Kirill and to please contact him, that he wants to start their chats again. But Kirill has gone stubborn about it and won't reply, for the moment anyway. It's a great story for Andy, he's landed on his feet and will be fine. I wish him all the best, but I'm really only interested in the ones who are left behind. Kirill was definitely left behind. The important thing is he knows we love him, and we all do. A kind Irish family have recently helped him open a small panel beating business in Russia, and we live in hope that the story will have a happy ending.

Recently Kirill sent me the most moving letter about what To Russia With Love has meant to him. Please remember that this letter was written by someone who has no formal education in English and no third level education. I think his fluency is remarkable under the circumstances:

The first time I meet Debbie in childhood orphanage when I was eight. When I was nine Debbie organised the trip to The Ireland for fourteen days, most of all kids went in to that trip. I don't have many memories of those holydays but I steel have a few and it just incredible. On that stage I wasn't even think that after two years she will organise the Charity To Russia With Love and will help to many people to try change theirs life and mine is well.

I can say a lot of things about Debbie but it's not enough to explain what she did exactly to me without knowing me and my character & I was very bold guy without the future and without the view of the own future. For years in my annual report I had the same record: 'the child is not amenable to rehabilitation.' I was very angry, quick-tempered, irritable and uncontrolled boy but Debbie always loved me even I was so bad. Gradually I begin to think about behaviour and actions but with such an examples as Debbie and all volunteers which stayed in orphanage I began to think a lot sooner than it could happen. Through constant communication with such good people gradually begin to love yourself a little, and others. Shifts were very small but still were and in 6th grade changes began. It was very difficult to deal with myself and with all the negativity that was in me. I knew that with such a character as I have I will not survive in the society.

By the end of 11th grade, I thought I was quite ready for independent living, but after a while I started to really realise that this is not the case. Now it is very difficult to describe the complexity of my life in those early years and understand the dramatic situations in which I got. The constant need for cash is very tempting to bad deeds. I have always lived with the thought of robbery and even murder, but the fear of the prison I was constantly stopped. Working in a different organisation, I did not get enough money to live and I often changed places of work.

I've always turned to Debbie for help. Debbie has never denied it, and it saved me from stupid acts and incorrigible situations. That words cannot describe when you realise that this period is over when you cannot manage emotions, and you're still free, and you have no sin. And the merit is of charitable organisations and in particular Debbie.

Now I found what I love and working to be professional in it. I'm doing Paintless Dent Repair and I hope that last moves to be happy. Thank You Debbie and thanks to Charity To Russia With Love.

12

HORTOLOVA – A FAMILY AFFAIR

If my whole family hadn't become deeply involved with Hortolova, I don't think I could have continued spending so much time there. As my children grew up, it became a big part of their lives, helped greatly by the fact that they were exactly the same age as some of our Russian orphans. They soon found that there was far more in common between them than anything holding them apart, despite the many material differences between lives in Clontarf and rural Russia. For years there have been regular letters from the children in Hortolova, back and forth, to my children, Trish's children, Marion's children and Paula's children. Our orphans love these relationships; they love reaching out to people over the walls.

Without wanting to sound like a complete do-gooder, I believe we should be teaching our children philanthropy from an early age, whether they like it or not. Otherwise we risk ending up with a generation of empty-headed Facebookers –

like the two blondes in the movie *Bruno* who have just been to a charity lunch 'for Darfur'. Bruno asks them, 'Have you thought about Darfive?' and they squeal, 'OMG, that's such a great idea …' It is incumbent on all parents to teach our children, in a meaningful way, that it's not our right to be indifferent just because, by a stroke of luck, we ended up being born here and not there. Even if they do it for the wrong reasons at first – because we force them, or because it's trendy, or whatever – something will eventually stick. After all, the world is both bigger and smaller than they think.

There have been many times that I have had to drag Mikey out of bed on a Saturday morning, because we have had a bag-pack in the local supermarket (we have done this for years – we pack the groceries and the customer gives us a donation; it's basically a bucket-rattle, with frills) and someone has let me down at the last minute. He might have grumbled furiously at the time, but he always did it, and I would hope that the legacy of that will stand to him through life. And for all the resentment at 9 a.m. on a Saturday morning, my three children acknowledge that Russia has brought so much to our house over the years. A buzz; interesting people; interesting stories; links with a wider world.

In a way, my children grew up with the children in the orphanage. So many of the orphans would come here on holidays – for Christmas, maybe down to Connemara for the summer. We choose who visits on a needs-most basis, which can be complicated and even seem unfair. Other organisations might select the prettiest and best-behaved children, which I can understand, but we don't. We pick the children who have had the most difficult time, the greatest trauma, or sometimes because they need medical help that isn't available to them in Russia. It is always heartbreaking to choose, because they all need and deserve so much. Recently, two of the bigger orphan boys came and climbed Carrantuohill with a group of volunteers – they were like mountain goats compared with the Irish.

Quite a few of the children have come to visit several times and are very much part of our household. This meant that when I was heading off to Russia my kids were happy, because they knew, for instance, that a kid who they were friends with would be getting a new pair of glasses from me and that this – with some strong-arming of relevant officials – would help keep him out of the blind orphanage. They were involved, on a profound level, with these Russian children and their lives. Sophie and Zina always knew all about the battles I was going to fight on behalf of particular children. Our conversations at the kitchen table always included the story of the day, the problems around it and how we might solve them. And they usually ended up with a profound and in-depth discussion of Cameron Diaz's make-up. Normal family, I would say. Mikey was too young at first, and of course he's a boy, so he doesn't absorb himself to that level, but he, too, was interested and his ears were always open.

And of course my mother, the ultimate Mrs Doubtfire, would arrive into the house every time I left, with a bag full of goodies, ready to spoil them all rotten. That made all the difference. And it has meant that my mother has had a huge relationship with my children, because she has minded them so often when I wasn't there, which is wonderful for them, for her and for me!

Sophie travelled out first when she was fifteen, having raised the necessary €3,000 herself, and has been out twice a year, every year, since. She has spent long summers at the orphanage as a volunteer and has close friendships with many of the children there. She still writes every week to the little ones and is on Facebook every day to our grown-up boys and girls. After school she studied education and training, and has also worked in orphanages in Bali and Thailand, so I think it's fair to say that To Russia With Love has shaped her interests in a really significant way. When she was doing work experience as part of her degree, she assisted at various schools, some posh, some disadvantaged, and found that her real passion lay with the disadvantaged. She had no interest at all in the lovely middle-class schools, because there wasn't enough of a challenge.

Mikey played basketball for Ireland last year, so the sport is high on his agenda. Last winter, in minus 24ºC, he went out to Russia with some of his team mates to coach our kids, who now regularly win all the local leagues. To raise the money they needed, the four Irish boys did a sponsored leg-and-chest wax – i.e., the girls from their school paid €50 each to tear a wax strip off them, as they howled in agony. They did such a bad job that Mikey had hair growing back in clumps all over his body for months!

In general I'm not a fan of the whole Transition Year trip abroad thing. Schools often ring us and enquire about it, saying it would be so good for their children. But I'm not interested in things being good just for Irish children – even though we could have made serious money if we had been less fussy, because there are huge fund-raising opportunities based around such trips. If it's of benefit to our Russian children, then yes, but if it's a bunch of Dublin kids who are going out to skip around and play with an orphan this afternoon, because tomorrow they're going sight-seeing, then no thanks.

Anyone who got near our children did so only if there was a meaningful reason for the contact. I have friends who criticise me for this, saying that their child got so much out of a trip to an African orphanage, say. But we don't let strangers in to play with our orphans. They can become circus animals all too easily, stared at by a group of affluent teenagers who are bussed in for a couple of days, then bussed out again, leaving our kids feeling envious and empty. One exception is a school who do this beautifully, Scoil Eanna in Rathfarnham; they have a wonderful ethos, wonderful staff, wonderful children. They fund-raise for Indian orphanages and also for us.

The women of To Russia With Love were spending so much time in Russia, that at one stage we decided to organise a husband's trip. Mick had already been over a few times – when we took Zina for her adoption interview with the judge and another trip to fix up her birth mother's wooden house – but some of the other husbands hadn't. They needed to be involved, because the charity was absorbing so much of their family life.

So off they went on their own, the five husbands of the five female directors. They paid for themselves, of course, and Igor had an itinerary. Of course. They had a hilarious trip. They went out in minus 25°C and I think were stunned by the kind of cold we work in. They did their *banya* – the traditional night-time sauna where everyone beats themselves with birch rods, rolls in the snow, then heats up with a shot of vodka – and generally had a fantastic trip. Igor brought them round all the orphanages and they met all the officials, who were delighted to wine and dine them, because here, finally, were the all-important men behind the women! But Mick has a very bad back and long flights are a misery for him. He won't even go to the cinema, because it's too much sitting, and he really doesn't relish travelling. During the adoption trip, an ambulance was organised to bring him to court, because it was two hours from where we were staying. Yet he never complains.

And anyway so much of Russia has come to our house over the years that he has been able to be deeply involved without leaving the country. He is very close to Kirill and some of the other boys who have come to stay. To them, it's unbelievable to see a man standing at the sink, doing the dishes. They can't believe that the man of the house would take on such a menial occupation. Good role models are needed for these boys, because they don't see enough of them.

Last Christmas, Kirill and Zina's friend Pasha were both here. Pasha stood up and made a wonderful speech on Christmas Day. Russians have a great tradition of speech-making, allowing them to praise, apologise, admire and inspire so eloquently. For all that they can seem intimidating and stern, they will then stand up and make the most deeply profound, emotional speeches, using the most wonderful words, straight from their hearts. We are a much more gregarious and outgoing nation generally, but when it comes to speech-making, I am always bowled over by the Russians. It has happened to us regularly at meetings over the years – a Russian official will suddenly launch into an exquisite speech, using poetry and literary quotations, and then it's our turn to try and match it by cobbling together some lines from James Joyce or W. B. Yeats.

There is one poem of Yeats' that we have used many times over the years, because it has always seemed so apt:

Had I the heavens' embroidered cloths,

Enwrought with golden and silver light,

The blue and the dim and the dark cloths

Of night and light and the half light,

I would spread the cloths under your feet:

But I, being poor, have only my dreams;

I have spread my dreams under your feet;

Tread softly because you tread on my dreams.

It is very relevant to our children, because they have laid their dreams under our feet. That is exactly what they did, once they began to trust us. And therefore, I'm not trying to be dramatic, but we do have to tread so carefully, not to crush those dreams.

13

SOULMATES

Zina has always had a romantic nature. She has a mirror ball in her bedroom that goes round every night and sprinkles magic light around the room. And I suppose she has every right to believe in fairy tales. The story of her life has so many strange, happy coincidences and twists of fate.

Pasha was the boy who originally brought me to Russia. He was Zina's friend from the baby orphanage where they had both spent their early years. Her protector, partner-in-crime and soulmate. They were bold when they were small, so they were always in trouble together. They got punished for the same things, locked out of classrooms, made to miss dinner. They had so much shared history that Zina couldn't bear being separated from him and kept asking me to find him after she came to live with us.

The sad irony was that, having gone all the way to Hortolova to find this boy, he wasn't there. Zina's entire class were, except for Pasha. It took us ten years to find him. He had gone out of the system – some said he'd been adopted by an American years earlier, but there was no paper trail so we couldn't verify that. As it happened, an unpleasant Russian farmer who lived in a small village had fostered him.

About four years ago, one of our staff, Inna, was in Bryansk college one day, where some of our children are students, and a young man walked up to her – unbelievably – and said, 'My best friend, Zina, went to Ireland many years ago, and I think you work for an Irish organisation? Can you please see if you can find this woman?' And he showed her a photo of me with Zina that he had been carrying round for years. Inna said, 'That's my boss ...'

The photo had been taken at the American ambassador's house here in Dublin, at a garden party. The remarkable thing is that Pasha was at that party too. He had come to Ireland the same summer as Zina, although we didn't then realise it, and had spent a month with a family not far from our home and been invited to the same garden party. Quite incredibly his Irish sponsor family had also made enquiries about keeping him, because they were mad about him, but they got nowhere with it and Pasha was sent back to Russia. The family tried many times subsequently to locate him, but were unsuccessful. He had by then been fostered and had fallen off the official radar. To this day, they have photos from his time with them in 1997. Funnily, Pasha is now a welder, just like the father of that family.

I phoned Pasha when next I was in Russia – he was stunned that this circle had finally closed. I went to meet him first without telling Zina. At that time she still had a photo of him in her bedroom and I knew how much he meant to her. I didn't want to get her hopes up, in case somehow things went wrong. As it turned out, Pasha was a lovely young man, beautifully dressed and well groomed. He had run away from his foster father aged fourteen and somehow learned to be a welder. At that stage he lived in a wooden hut somewhere, but looked after himself very well. He had nobody in the entire world.

We flew him in for Christmas two years ago. Zina still didn't know. For fifteen years she had been talking about this boy and hoping to find him. Actually, we should have told her, prepared her for what was coming. It was supposed to be a surprise, but it was too much to suddenly spring him on her. I realised this at the last minute and told her just before he came through the arrivals doors. He picked her up in his arms and wouldn't put her down.

It was a very strange time in our house …

Neither of them said anything the whole way home. The whole situation was overwhelming. Once home, Pasha pulled out a jewellery box with a tiny gold cross inside it for Zina. He had spent every penny he had on the present. She was just overcome by the whole thing. It was a very emotional experience. Zina clearly holds a special place in his heart.

Certainly he couldn't take his eyes off her. Zina meanwhile was delighted, teary and embarrassed all at once; she didn't know how to handle it.

We love Christmas in our house, every year is a huge fuss. Lights, candles, decorations, presents – and always a tree drama! We go to a Wicklow forest to buy one, often walking for miles with it, and then might easily pick up another one in Clontarf on the way home, if they turn out to be nicer. It's all part of the fun. But Zina has never loved Christmas, partly because she remembers the feeling in her tummy year after year, as she waited at the window of the orphanage, snow falling outside, for someone to visit her. Some orphan children did get visits, but very few. No one ever visited Zina. But also, she can't bear to see the huge piles of Santa presents under the tree here, when she knows so many little ones over there are waking up to nothing.

However, that particular Christmas was different. She had Pasha there. He was glued to her and she was showing him her life, but trying to play it down because he had so very little in comparison. It was extremely intense for both of them. Where do you start? I really didn't know.

On Christmas Day, as we served up dinner, Pasha stood up and made the most magnificent speech I have ever heard a Russian make – and by God, they do incredible speeches. He tried to describe how much he loved Zina, but even he couldn't really put words on it. He tried to explain the pain he felt when she didn't arrive back to the orphanage after the summer here, how he had left a message for her about where he was going when he was fostered in case she ever came back, but that none of the carers would listen to him. He said he thought about her every day while in foster care and focused on the one photo he had of her every night. He swore to himself he would find her again. He ran away at fourteen. All this we learned during his heart-breaking speech.

Pasha held himself together very well for the whole trip, until the last night. I went upstairs to help him pack – he had so many Christmas presents, from everyone I know, and couldn't fit them all into his case. There was music on, bloody *Titanic*, 'My Heart Will Go On'. I've hated it ever since. I was sitting on the bed beside him, wrestling with his suitcase and he started to cry. I'd say I got fifteen years' worth of tears in two hours. Everything from bereavement, to loss, pain and bullying. Zina couldn't look at him for hours afterwards, as she knew he had been crying. He was twenty, was heading back to a fairly miserable life, and both of their hearts were broken. I was at a loss – he was never going to live in Ireland and Zina was never going back to Russia. It was an impossible situation.

After that visit, we put Pasha in our Leaver's Programme. He went back to college to finish his education. He lived in one of our two flats in Bryansk and has since got himself firmly on his feet. He and Máirtín are great friends, they play the guitar beautifully together when Máirtín is in Russia.

Pasha has always been a lovely part of Zina's life. They still write to each other, letters that are so emotional and beautiful. He's getting married soon to a gorgeous Russian girl, as he feels the need to move on with his life. He has asked Trisha and me to go to the wedding as his surrogate parents, because he has no one else. He invited Zina too, but she has decided not to go, although she genuinely wishes him all the best.

Zina meanwhile has always planned her very own Big Fat Pink Gypsy Wedding. Oh God, we are all bracing ourselves for that day ... I'm guessing there will be mirror balls everywhere! In fact, she and Sophie have a deal done for many years – Sophie will design the wedding and Zina will be nanny to Sophie's children!

14

RUSSIA'S OPRAH, AND AFTER

Andrei Malakhov is a superstar in Russia, like Jerry Springer, Prince William and Brad Pitt all rolled into one. Fifty million people a week watch his show in Russia. So what was he doing in my kitchen in Clontarf other than enjoying Monny's apple tart?

Through a friend of mine, who owns the loveliest little tea shop in Moscow, Malakhov got wind of the work we were doing with To Russia With Love and became fascinated with the idea of this Irish woman, in the bowels of rural Russia, working with orphans. He decided he wanted me on his show, to do a special on orphans and adoptions, and why Ireland was having such a big impact on the children of his country. My idea was that I would do the show – I would tell my story, the whole of Russia would hear what we were doing and this would be of huge benefit to the charity.

First, Malakhov came to Ireland. He brought a full film

crew here for four days, came to our house for dinner, chatted with us all, loved our hospitality and relished my mother's apple tart. He was very sensitive to Zina and our story, and generally the loveliest person. Plus he's gorgeous. Unshaven, torn jeans, curly hair; deep, quiet and sensitive. But that's his off-screen look. Once he's on camera, it's make-up, blow-dry, the expensive suit and straight into TV-host mode. The show is akin to *Oprah* in appeal, but more Jerry Springer in style. It's a deliberately controversial show; everybody in Russia denies watching it, but somehow it racks up twenty million viewers a show, fifty million a week. It's constant shock-factor television. Russian TV is unbelievably corny at the best of times and this show is unashamedly sensationalist.

Andrei loved Ireland, he was blown away by Powerscourt waterfall, among many other places. He loved the ease of life here, the greenery, the castles and the antiques. Plus his absolute idol is Sinead O'Connor, so as a surprise we set up a meeting. He was in heaven. She was extremely nice to him and so that was the icing on the cake for his trip. The then lord mayor, Gerry Breen, could not have been more hospitable. He taught Andrei how to pull a pint in the Mansion House and invited him to switch on the Christmas lights in O'Connell Street. All the Russian women watching the ceremony mobbed Andrei – they were just stunned to see their biggest celebrity standing outside the GPO. In the end, we had to bundle him into a taxi and leave.

We had a funny moment in a small flower shop in Clontarf, where Malakhov went to buy a bouquet for Sinead O'Connor. The girl behind the counter was Russian and when she looked up to ask what flowers he wanted, she was struck dumb. A bit like me bumping into George Clooney in SuperValu I guess.

Russians love Malakhov. He challenges the system on occasion, and other times simply conducts probing interviews. He recently married a Russian beauty and together they are definitely the Wills and Kate of Moscow. You just don't expect to see him in Clontarf Flowers! I have had many long, deep chats with Andrei. He is caring, warm and gorgeous, but the in-built journalist comes out as soon as he's on air. His show is something else and he does it brilliantly.

While here, he interviewed Irish couples who have adopted Russian children, and was amazed at their warmth, their passion and the sense of family. He listened to my stories of our Russian children and couldn't believe the success we had with so many.

Following Andrei's trip to Ireland, I set off for Russia on our annual Santa trip, with a group of volunteers dressed as elves and of course Santa himself. The trip covers many institutions: orphanages, baby homes, shelters and so on. Trisha had us all whipped into red aprons and hats; Máirtín had his guitar out; carols were sung morning, noon and night; emotions were high and days were long.

At every place we visited, children were waiting with bated breath for Santa to get out of the minibus. Hundreds of them, with their faces pressed up against frosty windows, watching us arrive with sacks of presents to be distributed. I cannot describe the electricity in the air. It is an emotional, thrilling, sad and draining time. At that time of year, it is especially tragic to see so many little ones who have missed the adoption boat, and even Santa has to be watched carefully. Irish men are so soft, especially when it comes to children. At any moment, the man wearing the white beard and gold glasses is likely to break down, maybe because some tiny little thing is weeing on his knee with the excitement of it all. Or, as happened last time, because a little girl, just three years old, had been given to the orphanage that very day. She was terrified and clung onto Santa, whose big, white beard covered his tears; he knew she had thirteen more years there before her release date. Once you see Santa starting to cry, big tears rolling down behind the glasses, you have to take him out and get him to pull himself together.

Finally Santa took the elves home. Trish and I stayed on for Malakhov's TV show. I was absolutely at my most exhausted by that stage, a physical wreck. I had torn some ligaments in my knee a few months earlier and had an operation to fix the problem just before the Santa trip. Then, on the train from Moscow to Bryansk, I pulled my shoulder out of place. But

I was also on a high because I was sure the money was going to come pouring in as soon as Malakhov's show was aired. I genuinely thought we'd have €5 million in the bank the next day. Russia has a population of 142 million and many of them are incredibly wealthy. I was wondering how we would even spend all the money? What was I going to say to all the oligarchs who would want to help?

Although I have previously been on RTÉ and BBC, this was a whole new ball game. It was a huge studio, with endless lines of security to enter and fourteen or fifteen cameras. At that stage I hadn't seen the show, as we don't watch TV when we are in Russia, but I had met Andrei and was perfectly happy about it all. Igor, I have to say, didn't see the value in my doing this, but, nevertheless, as always, helped arrange all backstage matters once he saw I was determined.

My family had been flown in also, seated in the front row, and – much to Mick and Mikey's horror – plastered in tons of foundation. The audience had been packed out with children from the orphanage, going back twelve years. Malakhov interviewed many of them. They were so nervous and I was so proud of them. They were all dying to get in how the Irish had loved them and given them a chance at life. I was just sorry that they couldn't all get to speak.

The studio is set with a central sofa and three armchairs on either side. One lot of armchairs is filled with 'experts' who agree with the theories being aired, among them my great friend and Joycean expert Ekaterina Genieva; the other lot of chairs with more 'experts' who disagree. And Malakhov doesn't sit down and have a cosy chat with you. He stays standing, at the front of the stage, near the audience, and keeps things moving along, fast.

A few things happened during the show. Some of my older To Russia With Love children, who I hadn't seen in years, were brought on to surprise me and to tell their stories of what the Irish had done for them. Two of our great success stories were sitting beside me; one is an IT engineer, the other is going to be a doctor. There were a few inserts from couples who had adopted and their experiences, and then Zina came on, wearing a stunning knitted dress and looking fabulous.

She was slightly nervous and sat down beside me. But Zina loves doing TV, telling her story, because she feels it may help others, so she soon settled down. Malakhov was questioning her about her birth family. As far as Zina knew then, she had a sister, whom she had met, and a mother, whom she couldn't remember, but who had given her up as a tiny baby.

Now, we had all gone through so much to prepare for this show, across two countries, and I just presumed that Malakhov was going to keep it simple. It never occurred to me that there would be a 'surprise'. Although I suppose if I had been more familiar with the show, I would have realised

– there's always a surprise! By then, to a degree, adoption had become the dominant theme of the show, and To Russia With Love really isn't in the business of adoptions. I didn't want this slant because my main goal was to seek help for our children.

Anyway, first, one of Zina's carers from the baby orphanage was brought on; an old woman, minder of the little five- and six-year olds – Zina didn't have happy memories of her. They dug her up from somewhere and she came on saying, 'Oh Zina, you were always my favourite child …' Zina smiled beautifully and just acknowledged her. In truth she couldn't bear her. By then, I was beginning to realise that a huge amount of research of which we knew nothing, had gone into the show. I started to get nervous as to where it would go next.

Then Malakhov announced, 'Zina's brother, Vlad!' And in comes this humble-looking, farmer-type from a village; kind face, poor, sad, but smiling. We weren't prepared for it at all. He was shaking with nerves, and came and gave Zina two red roses wrapped in plastic and kissed her cheek. He was in his mid-forties and visibly overwhelmed, but he started to tell Zina bits and pieces about her family.

Vlad too was raised in an orphanage and the older sister, whom Zina and I had met five years previously, was in yet another orphanage. He told her that her father was a good man and that he had visited Zina once, bringing her a red scarf. Zina turned to me saying, 'I told you!' We must always have looked like we didn't believe her when she recounted that story, but she was right as it turned out. And so her father was immediately forgiven, on the basis of that one visit.

Zina was slightly in shock at the appearance of her brother and then Malakhov began talking to her about her birth mother, asking did she not want to meet her, would she not like to try to help her? Zina was trying to bat it off, saying, 'This is my mother,' and placing her hand on my arm, 'I don't have another one. One is enough,' and 'She was never there for me so I do not see her as my mother …' Looking back at the tape, I am so proud of Zina, who has grown into a very self-assured young woman. She was compassionate, but not prepared to be drawn into the drama of her early life so publicly.

The next thing a screen was dropped, and on it I saw the ramshackle, remote little village where Zina's mother lives. They had sent a camera crew to this godforsaken place. It looks like a village from a scary Russian fairy tale; six or seven wooden shacks, leaning to one side, around a pond with geese. It's an hour-and-a-half from the nearest road. Igor, Derek and I had gone there once – an unforgettable experience. We bumped across field after field in a Lada. And when we arrived, all the villagers stood gazing at us, because normally they see no outsiders.

They call them Wild People in Russia. They wear blankets and rough old boots. It truly is like something out of a dark fairy tale. Half of the year they have no electricity and no running water, they survive winters of minus 30ºC. They are truly a dying breed. Mick had been back there once, after my visit, to fix up Zina's birth mother's wooden cottage. After that, we cut all ties, because Zina really did not want us to be involved with her.

So there, on screen, was the ancient little village, and then a small house full of old women, including Zina's birth mother. Zina has no memories of her at all and suddenly here she is, on TV, part of Russia's biggest show.

I said to Zina, 'Don't look at the screen …' I took her literally under my arm at that stage, to shield her. She didn't want to see. She looked over towards Mick instead and was happy not to take part in this bit. I could hardly listen to what was being said, because my biggest fear was that Malakhov was going to say, 'And now, here we have Zina's mother!' and actually bring her into the studio. I was gesturing to Mick and he was gesturing back to say, 'There's an exit there, take Zina off stage.' We would just have walked off – I was not prepared to have my daughter meet her birth mother on national television. In fact, this was never Malakhov's intention, and the show moved on.

However, he did have one more surprise in store. Malakhov had Pasha, Zina's soulmate, the boy we had searched for for ten years and finally found just a few years earlier, brought out.

He held Zina's hand and Malakhov asked him would he like to say anything to her.

Pasha was nervous but spoke up: 'I want to say to you, in front of all of Russia, that I love you. It is the first time I have ever used the words.'

'What would you like to say back to him?' Malakhov asked.

Zina sat up, dignified and gorgeous. 'That's nobody's business but ours! I'll tell him privately what I have to say to him, certainly not here!'

Sophie, Mick and Mikey all spoke about Zina and how easy the years have been for us together. They looked gorgeous, and I was so proud of them all, because I know they were only there to help the charity.

Before the cameras stopped rolling, I took the opportunity to make a request: 'Andrei, you didn't ask me what I wanted for Christmas … I'm not able to carry the weight of these orphan children any more. My wish is that I find some Russian people who want to help, because Irish people can't carry this burden any longer.'

After the show, everything was bedlam. It's not like the green room in RTÉ with ten people chatting quietly; there are hundreds of people milling around, in a massive TV station. There were so many of our children, going back years, which was also very emotional. They were coming out of the audience to greet me; the 'experts' were coming up to me to continue the debate – pro-adoption? anti-adoption? – I was holding Zina by the hand. Sophie was hugging our To Russia With Love children and Mikey was trying to wipe the make-up off his face. Meanwhile one of the adoption 'experts' was asking Zina for her number. We did talk to her brother, but not much. His bus was leaving. He gave us his number and asked that Zina please contact him, but she hasn't. She doesn't want to, so I'm not going to pursue it. If she wanted to, I would be the first to follow the whole thing up.

When the show was aired, on Russian Christmas, which is 6 January, my appeal at the end was edited out. I couldn't believe it. Once I knew I was going on Andrei Malakhov's show, I was so sure that all our problems were solved. I was sure I would find oligarchs falling in love with our story and with what we were doing, longing to help, throwing money at us, but I didn't find that at all. After the show, all we got were hundreds and hundreds of emails into the office, requesting help. We got begging letters for months, but very few donations.

Andrei tried his best to help by airing our plight, but couldn't in the end include my appeal and so our reasons for doing the show came to nothing. I wasn't there to display the Deegans, we were all there together – me, the To Russia With Love children and my family – with the hope that funds would flow and many would benefit. This sadly did not happen.

Ultimately, Andrei's show was a kind of tribute, a *This*

Is Your Life-type show, for Zina rather than the straightforward interview we had been expecting. However, he gave our children a voice that night. He let me tell my story. He let Russia hear how the Irish are changing children's lives, so the only regret for me was that my appeal was cut. I came across as a wealthy foreigner, who helps as a hobby, instead of the way I needed to come across – someone who badly needs Russian assistance to sustain this charity. Nevertheless, since the show I have been reminded again and again of just how much influence Malakhov has. Everywhere I go in Russia my path is smoothed by the fact that I know him and have been seen on air with him. Doors have opened for me because of this that never would have otherwise. For this, I am grateful. Also, he was incredibly complementary about Ireland at the start of the show and as a result many Russians are planning to visit our country!

Zina, because she is so grounded, so loved, happy and stable, was well able for the drama of it all. In fact, as it happened, it was me, who always thinks I can cope with anything, who wasn't.

The bottom line was I failed to raise funds for our children. In general Russian people do not trust each other or foreigners, and this is why they don't give like the Irish do. But I felt I could convince them. I truly failed. That, combined with my physical ailments, brought me to my knees in January 2011.

I had what I suppose you could call total burnout. I'm still in denial, so I don't know what to call it. However, you get away with nothing in our house, so I am regularly reminded of how awful I looked! They must get their shallowness from me ... But burnout it was.

I feared at that point that I couldn't find any more money in Ireland and suddenly it looked as though I couldn't find it in Russia either. My heart had been set on getting help from there, probably more than even I realised. When it didn't happen, I just didn't have the energy to keep going. I somehow got through Christmas and then I crashed in January.

I don't think I moved off the couch for six or seven weeks. I sat and watched the Shopping Channel all day, but I didn't shop. I never put on make-up – always a bad sign, as normally I wouldn't go to the Spar without it. I stayed in the same clothes, t-shirt and leggings, in bed and out. I didn't go outside the door, I didn't want to see people. I guess it was fourteen years of an emotional rollercoaster also taking their toll. The journeys back and forth across time zones, the endless worry and upset and elation of all those years, must suddenly have hit me.

My biggest fear was, who is going to tell the children? Who is going to break it to them? They are so dependent on us. This dependency is a key part of our success. Without the level of involvement we have, there is no way these children, from squalid, difficult, dysfunctional backgrounds, could ever go on to have decent, normal lives – let alone become doctors, lawyers and accountants.

One day, I just got tired of myself. I'd worn a hole in the sofa at that stage. It was time to get up and get on with it. Really, I can't stand moany people. I didn't get any fixing, although I suppose that was the time, if ever, that I needed a therapist. Luckily, I have an incredible group of friends and they were all watching the situation. Grainne, my BF and the polar opposite to me – a listener, wise and as good as any therapist – was on the job. My mother too. Dinners were arriving, housework was being done around me. So I got up off my ass and switched my lights back on. Once March arrived and the daffodils started to pop out, I pulled myself together. God bless spring.

I got myself back on my feet and thought, to hell with it, we've got to get back out there and start fund-raising again. A few weeks later I went on Brendan O'Connor's *Saturday Night Show*, hoping it would be a huge success. On the Sunday morning after the show, I checked for texts with the €5 I had asked for. My email showed three complaints from people who couldn't get through. I was gutted again – three people had tried to donate and failed! The next day I went to the office, tail between my legs, only to discover that more than 25,000 people had got through and donated. We had €140,000 in donations after it, half-a-year's funding in one night. Only three people hadn't got through! My faith was restored. We were back and fighting thanks to Brendan being bold with our text campaign details and Zina sitting beside me looking fab once again and happily telling Brendan, who she loves, her story. She is rightly so proud of who she is and everything she has achieved.

That showed me that there is still goodwill and hope. It relit the fire within me. I thought, here's little Ireland again, funding us. The Irish people, as always, showing unbelievable generosity. That inspired me to keep going.

15

WHERE TO NOW?

We didn't see the recession coming. I don't know that anybody did; it seemed to just hit like a ton of bricks. And To Russia With Love was affected immediately. The donations started to dry up, almost overnight.

By 2009 we were entirely dependent on public generosity. No more funds were coming from the Irish government because Russia by then was flexing its muscles, no longer a poor country – though try telling that to the 347,000 orphans. Although we got a hefty grant from the EU six years ago – €250,000 – it was a one-off, and we spent every penny, as agreed, on a huge re-socialisation programme, basically meaning the normalisation of each element of a child's life, from food choices to sporting activities. The aim was to train them for the outside world. The hoops and barrels one has to jump through for an EU grant are unbelievable, but well worth the trouble.

We had always known that there would come a day when ordinary people would begin to say, 'Hang on, Russia is a wealthy country, why are we supporting their orphans?' When Roman Abramovich bought Chelsea Football Club and we were still out there asking for money for Russian children, it seemed so ridiculous. However, despite the obscene wealth in evidence, Russia has two very distinct tiers of society – the very rich and then everybody else, who are, many of them, barely surviving. Below that again, are the orphans. Change is coming. President Putin has plans, some good people in the system are rattling cages and calling for a stop to institutional care. But the country is so vast and poverty so endemic that it will take a long time. And our orphans are at the bottom of the waiting list.

Once the recession hit, that anomaly affected us immediately. Ireland was suddenly much poorer and Russia visibly much richer. We found it very difficult very quickly. We were very 'events based', meaning balls, lunches, golf days and so on, and these events became box-office poison. Our last ball was three years ago and we thought selling tickets would be like pulling teeth. In fact, it wasn't, but we knew we couldn't risk it again. What made it all the harder was that we had started To Russia With Love at the beginning of the Celtic Tiger, so our fund-raising norm was as distorted as everything else at the time. We were used to selling tickets, golf classics, ladies' lunches, all effortlessly. Once cut-backs really hit Ireland – fewer support teachers, cystic fibrosis sufferers with no wards to go to, home carers cut, people on the radio every day lamenting the hardship – we fully understood we were pushing water up a hill.

I began feeling guilty myself, asking people for money when I knew the children in Crumlin Hospital didn't have the right facilities. I found it far more difficult, because I felt people were struggling in their own lives and struggling to find the bit extra to give to Irish kids who needed help. Even so, I still believe that if Irish people trust you, even if they are on their knees, they will always give you a fiver. We are totally unique as a nation; extraordinarily generous.

Three years ago the board of To Russia With Love sat down and said, 'Is this sustainable? We can't be making promises to donors if we can't see them through.' We have been battling for three years now to keep the organisation alive. I've thought of opening a charity shop – we are actually looking at premises at the moment and it could be a successful plan. I love the idea of a gorgeous one, plus my own training and background are in retail, as part of the management team in Mirror Mirror (those over forty will remember!). All charities are scrambling for ideas at the moment. There aren't many creative ways left to raise money.

We have huge relationships with very small children who are heavily dependent on us. That's the problem for me now. For the first time, I can't reassure them that we're always going to be here. In the last few months I have even tried to wean myself away from visiting so much. Because the more I visit, the more I get to know our new children and the harder it is.

Some people will always believe I'm only in it for myself; for the good PR, the claps on the back. In fact, some have even gone so far as to say it to me. If that was true, I might have lasted a couple of weeks, maybe a year or two. Not fourteen years. When you get an award and everyone says, 'Oh, you're amazing', yes, there's a buzz to that – a huge buzz; I'm as shallow as they come and I love that bit of it – but it doesn't get you through interminable building meetings where you're discussing tiling for five hours, or collecting the body of a child you love from the morgue. It doesn't even get you through the seven-hour train journey, standing on a windy platform with the icy cold biting your skin, knowing you have left home yet again, that you have ten days of gruelling hard work in front of you, with difficult, damaged children. And it certainly doesn't keep you going when the money dries up and everyone is telling you that the sensible thing is to quit. Loving the notion of yourself as one of the good guys simply isn't enough when the times get as tough as they are now.

When I was honoured as Rehab International Person of the Year in 2009, one of my closest friends and mentors rang me and said, 'What you need to do now is to close the organisation down. Leave on a high note.' He could see the recession coming. Even so, I couldn't understand it – why? Just so I could go out in a blaze of glory? I said, 'I can't leave the kids.' How selfish would that have been? I'm not saying I'm not unbelievably selfish about other things, just not that particular thing. I couldn't do it, even though he was probably right. He suggested I go into politics – I thought that was funny, as my school principal used to say the same. I think I'd rather sleep with Gary Glitter.

On the night of the award itself, which is a really big deal – 750 people having a black-tie dinner in Citywest, with the president, Mary McAleese, in the front row and my mother feeling that this was her proudest moment – Grainne Seoige brought Brendan O'Connor on stage to present me with my award. A wonderful moment, if you didn't have to walk up steps in eight-inch heels, with cameras on you and Brendan doing his usual slagging: 'Here she is … Bob Geldof with a rack!' Actually, he's super because he relaxed me completely, even though I wanted to kill him for the boob comment!

Now, we'd been warned by the organisers not to do any pitching from the stage, but I knew the show was being broadcast live, that once I was up there, they couldn't do anything to stop me, so I said to Brendan, 'Between us, we need to get across that To Russia With Love badly needs money.' I wasn't going to miss such a golden opportunity. I knew everybody in Ireland would be watching, so I gave Brendan the nod and he said – heroically, because he too knew it wasn't allowed – 'How can we help?' I said, 'Well, if everybody texted five euro to ...' and I gave the donation number we had set up. At that stage, if a hook could have come from backstage and dragged me off, it would have. But within twenty minutes we had €60,000 in donations. Yet again, the Irish people proved that if you ask, they would give.

After the show I was brought into a room at the back, with my award in my hands, and told off in a nice way. They are great people actually and I am very proud of my award. But I always believe it's better to look for forgiveness than permission. Certainly in this case.

However, in general, once the country was in recession, I lost the will to ask ordinary people. I thought more multi-nationals might get involved instead, so we decided to open a Moscow office and go after Russian corporate money. We started To Children With Love in Moscow, a separate en-tity legally, with a separate board. We are trying to tap into the Corporate Social Responsibility funds of the big interna-tional companies based there. I have a super board member, Gerry Loughrey, who is a CSR expert, and he and I tackle the Moscow companies together. It's a job and a half, but, slowly, it seems to be working. Not without headaches though. The main problem is that these companies are very nervous of who they give their money to, because there is so little transparency in Russia. Once we get in front of them and convince them, they do seem to want to help. But it is a slow burn. Working in Russia is not at all what we are used to in the West. It's a completely different ball game and you need to understand the rules very well, or you lose the will to live very early on.

For example, one caveat I keep hearing is: 'We'll pay for projects but not staff.' I never understand that. Who's going to pay the staff to run the projects? You can't separate the administration from the minding. These companies want to be able to tell their shareholders that the money is only going to the children. But if you don't have excellent governance, you don't have excellent programmes and transparency. And to get excellent governance, you don't bring in a volunteer for two hours on a Monday morning. You don't run international banking corporations like that, so why would you run a charity this way? For some reason, some people expect charities to be home-spun, with a biscuit tin for money, and kind people who knit while answering the phones for no pay.

This is not the case. The volunteers who get on a plane and go to our orphanages in Russia are amazing, and we have had a few wonderful, absolutely dependable people over the years in our office in Dublin. Angela Kelly was our pro-bono bookkeeper for years until she retired. But it would be hard find another one like her because, in general, clever staff cost money.

We have come across some remarkable people and organisations in Moscow, such as Kellogg's, who have a genuine philanthropic view on things and are rounded partners, not just cheque writers. They support a superb scholarship programme working with some of our more able children, a large food donation programme, and their management team have visited many times. Kellogg's really know how to make a difference. More companies need to emulate them!

The Marriott Group also helps us in many ways. Some of the hotels in Moscow have To Russia With Love collection boxes in their foyers. Recently they took up all the carpet from one hotel, because they were getting new carpets, and sent the old ones – still in very good nick – to us. Next they will donate old bedroom furniture, and just a couple of weeks ago some of our children were in the kitchens there, being trained by the Marriott chefs. It gave them a day out and some may well decide they want to work in a kitchen after the experience.

Avril Conroy, a powerhouse of a woman and central to the Irish community in Moscow, has been extraordinarily good to us. She moved to Russia more than eighteen years ago for her job, is a successful businesswoman and a tireless worker for children, who has given us the huge benefit of her experience and connections.

Last Christmas an English-language nursery school, ENS, attended by the children of well-heeled Russians, bought beautiful gifts for all our children, gorgeous presents, wrapped in expensive gold paper with great bows of ribbon. It made me smile, as usually they would get shampoo, a deodorant, some fruit or a selection box. But a little spoiling can do no harm. ENS also supplied some of our welcome packs (see Appendix A). We need more Russians like the wonderful woman who runs this beautiful little school – organised, trusting, kind and a real beauty.

At the moment, we have about a few more months' money in the bank. After that, we don't know where we'll be.

Meanwhile, children are still arriving into orphanages, a steady stream, although not on the same scale thank God. In the next decade, I hope we will see it peter out. The Russians are making the right noises, finally, about residential care. The Russian ombudsman of children's rights recently said that the dismantling of children's homes should be the task for the next five years. I suspect it will be longer than that, but hopefully we'll be around to see that happy day. I would love to be there when they turn the last key in the door of the last orphanage. In the meantime, we still have small children who will never be adopted. And I'd love to think that for the next five years at least we could be there, standing behind them.

We need €250,000 a year to survive, on a bare minimum, to continue our many wonderful programmes. That's a million and a quarter for five years. With that, we could see out what we started, instead of being forced to leave before it's over, which would be such a shame, because we've had such an impact. Not just in changing children's lives, but with trainers going out to Russia – foster care experts, residential care experts, institution experts – and teaching our best practice to the local staff. Russians love that part of it. They are so well educated – it seems everyone has a PhD in Russia – and they love learning from other people in their field, swapping information, hearing about standards and procedures. There are social care programmes being introduced on a wider scale that originated in our orphanages, with our staff training others in how to administer them.

At one stage Derek Tracy formed a board with the Russian governors of thirty-four different orphanages. We sat at meetings with these men and women, and they would listen to Derek talking, describing how things work here and internationally, and all of them scribbling furiously. At the time we were working with just one orphanage, but these directors all had more than 100 staff each, so you're talking about an effect on thousands of people.

One deputy governor, a woman, put it best in an email to me some years ago after a visit to Ireland. She said that the biggest impact the Irish had in her region was that we changed how Russian professionals looked upon the children. We changed their hearts and minds, because of the commitment we had. It wasn't just about building programmes – they actually began to see children as small humans and real people rather than state statistics.

At one stage we were going into the Department of Education in Bryansk almost every day, battling over individual children. At first, they thought we were arriving for lunch or a photo opportunity. I'd say, 'No, we're here because Lena was moved yesterday and she shouldn't have been moved, and we have to get her back.' They were fascinated that we actually knew these children's names. Again and again we brought up details and stories of individuals who were being damaged in their system, and eventually they started to listen. We wore them down with it. We eventually convinced key players to come round to our way of thinking. That was a big mind-shift for civil servants in an environment like Russia where they are so paper-driven and so far from the situation on the ground.

We didn't originally intend to do that. We wanted to mind children, not change the world. Fourteen years ago people were criticising us for rebuilding orphanages instead of agitating to close them down. And I could have become an advocate for children's rights, to fight for more advanced change. But in my heart, I didn't want to do that. I wanted to make sure that the four-year-old girls had a buggy with a doll in it, that they had a toothbrush and could brush their teeth. And if the same little one was grieving for a separated sister or brother, that we could reunite them. However, because of the level of our input and the extent to which we involved ourselves in Russian life, as a side line we did actually become advocates for change. The pebble we threw in had enormous ripples.

Only recently a Moscow newspaper described how 'the Soviet-era orphanages may have been patched up since the crisis years of the early 1990s, but they continue to stunt and damage children's development'. We first arrived during those crisis years, and what we found shocked us into action. Things have changed for the better and we have been part of that journey, but there is still a long way to go. The same newspaper report revealed that, 'A baby in a nursery may meet 120 adults in a year, but has less than ten minutes of real interaction a day with any of them.'

No wonder that the national statistics on orphan girls and boys are so shocking. Prison, prostitution, trafficking, crime, homelessness, babies being put back into care. Almost none of ours have gone through that process. They are minded, nurtured and parented, and as a result, they become stronger adults for their own community. I wish we could do more of this.

We have an extremely bright little girl at the moment, Anastasia. She has family members in Russia but they have no interest in her. She's eleven, bright as a button, a razor-sharp mind. Three years ago I would have had a programme waiting for her. I would have spotted her for university and she would be on her way now via our Challenger Programme. But at this point in time, I can't commit to that with her. I'm afraid to start something I can't finish, so I'm making her no promises. I'm nearly ignoring her, which is so unlike us as an organisation. She's a classic case of the children whose plight really bothers me. It's such a waste, there is so much potential lost. Anastasia knows what some of the older children got in terms of extra resources, and she and the other bright, ambitious children are asking, 'What can we get? Where are you now?' It's so difficult to say to them, 'The economy in Ireland is not allowing us to do it.' I haven't told the kids yet; I keep going to Moscow, trying to beat down the corporate doors, hoping I'll find someone to be my knight in shining armour. But they are very difficult doors to beat down. Hopefully, one or two will hear our story and wish to make a difference.

If the worst happens, yes, we can all walk away and go back to real life. I don't know what I'd do – take a year off and scrub floors in an ashram maybe? I'd never last, I need my roots done too often!

Recently I climbed a mountain in Wicklow with about ten friends. We were about 800 feet up, with about another 100 feet to go. I was exhausted, and asked, 'Have we still got to climb that last bit? I can't believe it ...' Mick, my husband, said, 'Turn around and look back down at what you've already climbed.'

'Why?'

Mick said, 'I always take great comfort from what I have achieved, rather than only looking at the bit I still have in front of me.'

'Well I never do. I don't care how far I've come, only how far I have to go,' I said.

If I could just look back on the wonderful stuff we've done over fourteen years, all the memories and the amazing people I've met, that would be lovely. But that 100 feet to the summit is still there and it's all I can see. Five, maybe ten, more years. We need to finish what we started, finish the journey that began with a little girl asking, 'Papa?', and then telling me about the children from her previous life, whom she missed so much. A promise to another little girl that I would come back and kiss her on her birthday. Thousands of promises every day since, to thousands of children who depend on us and on the extraordinary generosity of the Irish people for every good thing in their lives. Promises that I can no longer make.

It has been a difficult, at times dangerous, journey. Fourteen years of incredible highs and lows, from the elation of successfully raising €150,000 in one night, to the tragedy of burying four beautiful children. We have attended graduations, been to weddings, seen babies born and steps towards independence taken. Most of it has been simply the quiet glow of satisfaction when a heartbroken child smiles at last, when one with low self-esteem stands tall, when a child with a gift for learning scores the grades to take them to university and a better life.

Derek Tracy used to say, 'Don't forget lads, we get more out of this than any of us have ever given.' And he's right. The joy we have had from our Russian children over the years is incredible. And it has all been thanks to the generosity of Irish people.

This whole story has been extraordinary and the best bit is we are all so ordinary.

Today as I type this, I'm texting with the other hand. Another Irish angel is on the end of the phone, a great man, Cathal Lyons, who lives in Moscow and has just decided to climb Croagh Patrick to raise money for To Russia With Love. It's not an easy climb, and even trickier if, like Cathal, you only have one foot, following a motor bike accident. We cannot continue the work of To Russia With Love without the heroism of people like this, and the ordinary decency of everyone else.

The journey isn't over. The summit is in sight. We need help to get the children to the top of the mountain.

I know how difficult things are at home for everyone right now and I know I am like an LP with the needle stuck in the same groove, but if you can donate in any small way to allow us to finish what we have started, the children would be eternally grateful. Your donation will allow them have a fuller life and contribute to society in a meaningful way. I will continue to chase corporates, businesses and leave no stone unturned, but if you have read this far, you will hopefully feel our need. All donations add up, no matter how small. Please trust us to use your donation wisely, and do what we Irish are brilliant at, looking after children around the world who need our help, no matter where they are.

Please go to our website at

www.torussiawithlove.ie to donate.

Thank you.

16

FALLING IN LOVE, WITH A FAMILY

Zina's Story

For all that I feel Irish and part of a family, I know that there is another life out there that could have been mine ...

On my first trip to Ireland, as a seven-year-old, I didn't know what to expect. In the orphanage they told us nothing. They didn't tell me where I was going, who I was going to, what to expect, how long I was to be there, nothing. They didn't tell me I was going on a plane – and that wasn't even the strangest thing! That day was my first time on a bus and in a car, never mind a plane. So there were a lot of emotions going through my mind. I was a seven-year-old girl, I'd never been in a vehicle or out of the orphanage before, so there were a lot of nerves. We all had to look after each other on the trip. Because the staff weren't telling us anything, we children had to try to work it out for ourselves and get through each challenge as it came. We were going to the unknown, so all we could do was hope for the best.

When we arrived at our destination, we didn't know if it was our destination. There was no one telling us 'you have arrived'. We could easily have been passed on yet again to someone else. By then, I was exhausted. We walked down the tarmac, and Mick and Debbie were waiting for us there. I was so tired, I think I would have gone to anybody. I was so vulnerable at that stage, I didn't know what else to do; anyone who put their arms out, I would have gone to them. I was so tired of looking after myself.

I remember putting my hand on Mick's shoulder and asking, 'Papa?' It was a very clear moment. I had never said the word 'papa' in my entire life. Then and there, in that second, it felt so right. I thought, 'Yes, this is when I should be using it. Saying it to a person who I have never met.' It just clicked. I believe it was destiny.

I had no English, Mick and Debbie had a few words of bad Russian. They tried their best, I'll give them that! The first few days in their house, I was very uncertain of myself. I didn't know what to do. In the orphanage, it's like the army. There's a time for everything, so when I came to this house and they weren't telling me exactly what to do, when to eat, when to play, when to sleep, I felt very lost. Debbie always said to me, 'My house is your house', and I would say, 'No, my house is completely different.' It was only when she got to know the orphanage that she really realised that.

I don't remember anything from my life before the orphanage, but I remember the endless routine there. To this day, I still like structure and routine. Some days it was easier to accept than others. You learned what to do and the consequences of not doing it, very fast. If you put your foot out of line, you'd be put back into that line. I think it made me see the world differently – that there are boundaries, there are restrictions and that you need them. In the orphanage we were told what to do, what to say, what to wear, all the time. Everything was labelled and framed.

So I didn't know what a choice was. Still to this very day I find it very hard to make choices, because I didn't get that training as a child. Seven years is a long time not to be given the opportunity to choose anything, no matter how small. I still always ask advice from everybody else and I don't listen to my own heart.

I question myself and am never certain. I never learned and now I don't think I can learn. I've been told how to do it – to feel with your heart – but I don't know how to; I don't trust my instincts.

Back then, if someone said, 'Pick one', I would be thinking, pick it when? What colour? I would be panicking. These shoes or those shoes? I didn't know.

It was great to have Valya with me, because we figured it out together. For example, we didn't know what the sea was.

'What is this?' we wondered. 'What do we do with this?' We saw Sophie and Mikey taking their shoes off and running into the water. We were wondering, 'Is that natural? Is that what you're meant to do?' Really, Sophie and Mikey taught me how to be a child. To be free, not to worry what was coming next, to just let it be, to enjoy that moment. They didn't know they were doing it, but that's what they did.

After the first few difficult days, I loved it, but I wasn't letting myself love it too much, because I knew I was going back. I knew even then that once things go up, they always have to come down. As a seven-year-old, I felt I couldn't put my heart too much into this new life, because I knew leaving it would rip me apart and I didn't know if I was strong enough to deal with that. I had dealt with enough pain in my life, so I was very cautious.

But at times I was very vulnerable and so I gradually let Debbie, Mick, Sophie and Mikey in. I would think, 'I can't show you this part of myself, because I'm afraid this will happen.' But there were times when I couldn't resist, when I broke down and said, 'I don't want to go. I'm loving this, I know this is right, I feel this is right.' My mind was telling me, 'Don't put your heart in, because you will be going back', but I couldn't always listen. A child shouldn't be saying that to herself. But you learn to deal with things differently in an orphanage, you're more cautious, you're afraid to dip your toe in the water. That's how I am to this day – cautious.

I still have the feeling that I will have to drop down from heaven at some time. The irrational fear that it will all be taken away from me. And I think I'm still learning what love is. I'm twenty-three and every day I learn to love someone else and let someone love me. It's a process.

Those first weeks showed me that there was a different, better world outside the gates of the orphanage, with more things than I had ever realised. Seeing that made me understand, you can get what you want, you can get a mam and a dad and a family. Knowing that gave me hope.

I got meningitis, and while I recovered, Debbie and Mick put me into school. I had friends, I started doing sports, playing on teams. Eventually I realised, 'That's it, I'm here for good. There's no sending me back.' I was swimming, running, dancing. I just wanted to be really social. To this day, I love being busy.

Learning English was very hard though. I had a special teacher at school and, when I came home, another teacher to help me with my homework. Even without English though, I could communicate with some people. Like Monny, my Mam's mam. We didn't speak the same language, but we understood each other. We didn't have to use sign language; it was such a very strong bond, immediately. When my Mam started going to Russia, that bond just got stronger and stronger. Even now,

I'm incredibly close to Monny, I tell her everything, she's one of my favourite people in the world.

I still wonder, how did I learn English, learn to be a daughter, a sister, make friends, go to school, all in a year?

Bonding with Sophie was easy, because, in my mind, she was like another orphan. All the children in my class were the same age and I was used to having very strong bonds with them. In an orphanage, that's how it happens. With Mikey, I was like another mother to him, because when you're older in an orphanage, you learn to look after the younger ones. When I was six and seven, I was looking after the one- and two-year-olds. So when I came into the family, I thought, 'I'm doing this role!' I felt so safe and knew exactly what to do. It felt natural. I needed that role, and it was one I was very happy with and confident in. Me and Mikey were really close. I knew when to change him, when to put his socks on, when to give him his bottle. Now I'm a professional nanny and I love my job.

The hardest part was learning how to handle my emotions, even simple ones. I remember it was Sophie's birthday one year, and she was getting presents, and I found that very hard. I was thinking, 'What's going on with me? Why am I not getting presents?' I got jealous very quickly. Dealing with these emotions was hard, because I had always kept them in. When something happened, I'd be very quiet. I couldn't handle it and so I would just shut it off.

Managing my emotions made every day a challenge. Even taking turns speaking was hard – in Russia, everyone just shouts all the time, but in a family, you have to learn to speak in turn, not to demand stuff and not to go off in a huff when things don't go your way. I had to learn that it was okay to feel what I felt and that at the end of an argument, you kiss and hug and make up.

The family understood. Sometimes I'd have a tantrum, especially when I was ten and eleven, which were hard years for me. My dad would go upstairs with me and say, 'Sit here, count to ten, come back down and everything will be okay.' And it was. Thanks to that, I knew how long I had and what I had to do afterwards. In Russia a tantrum could go on for two weeks, because you didn't know how to resolve the situation. Children need a bit of help with that, they need to learn what to do with the rage.

Our house in Clontarf is pure mad. I think the door is going to run away one of these days – it opens and closes so much. It's busy, busy, busy. There's always some drama. I might wake up in the morning and there's one drama going on, by the time I come home in the evening, there are twelve more.

However, even with all the new things I was learning and how happy I felt, I missed the other children from the orphanage. They were my life for seven years. They were like an anchor. My bedroom in Russia was always full of children. You were never alone. In the bathroom, kitchen, school, there was always someone to talk to and play with. At home in Dublin, I was in a big room, on my own. It used to take me a very long time to get to sleep, because I didn't hear the other children talking or coughing. You get so used to the sounds. I think that was the loneliest part.

In an orphanage, you soon learn to depend on other children. You don't have many adults around you to observe, so you watch other orphans. We learned from each other – what to do and what not to do. I couldn't tell you one adult role model I had as a child. The carers didn't know anything about social and emotional development. They weren't trained in those areas. They didn't hug or kiss us. It wasn't their way. Some of them weren't interested in children and were only doing it for the money. Loving and caring were what we learned from each other. I remember there was a little girl, very young, who had a bad headache one day. She didn't know what it was and I didn't know anything, except to hug her and hold her head and rock her. I didn't know there were tablets for such things. She fell asleep and when she woke, it was gone. For all my wonderful new life, I was missing these children terribly and asking after them. So one day Debbie decided, 'I'll go and find them', and that's where it all started.

Pasha was the one I missed most. We grew up together. We were closer than the others; really, really close friends. We were so passionate about each other. He showed me emotions like love, caring, gentleness. I learned those from him and he learned them from me. I can't do justice to it. I would have loved for him to be adopted, so he could share the same life as me.

The other boys would sometimes gang up on the girls and hit us. If I got attacked, Pasha would step in immediately. He was very protective. He just knew, instinctively, to take care of me. And if he was hurt, I learned that my job was to take care of him, wrap up the cut or whatever.

One time, he got into trouble. He didn't behave himself, so he was forbidden to have dinner. I knew he'd be starving, so I hoarded all my food for the day and gave half to him. That's the way we looked after each other. We'd steal food from the kitchen together.

I think I still feel guilty that I got adopted and he didn't. I feel terrible. I'm twenty-three now, but I think when I'm forty-three, or sixty-three, I'll still feel the same way. Is it survivor's guilt? I don't know. But I do know it's very hard to say to him, 'I've done this, that, the other', because I don't want to be bragging. I don't think Pasha and I are as comfortable with each other as we were. But no matter what happens, I think we'll always have that childhood bond. Once you make that bond, I think it's unbreakable. We still keep in touch all the time.

Debbie didn't find Pasha when she went to Hortolova. He

had been fostered out. It was only years later that he came across one of the To Russia With Love carers and tracked us down. That he did shows me that we were meant to be together, to see each other again.

When Mam told me she had found Pasha and that he was coming to stay with us one Christmas, I was shocked. I wept. I don't know if I was crying for him, for our childhood, because I have a life and he doesn't, or what. There were a lot of emotions to deal with. When he came over, I didn't want to see him. I didn't know how I was going to do it. I didn't want to show him the life that I had and he didn't. The guilt was so strong.

I'm not a fan of going back to Russia. I find it very difficult, emotionally draining. After a trip there, I come home and sleep for a week; it takes so much out of me. When I'm in Russia, I love being there, but I still have the fear that if I stay too long, I'll never come home. I think crazy things, like Mam might forget to pay for my ticket or something. I get panicky a lot in Russia, I'm not myself, I'm on edge all the time. So much so that I tire myself out. Moscow is fine, it is away from the smells of my childhood. But when I go to Bryansk, I can't handle it. It's just everything about the place. I'm never prepared for it.

Last year, I was on Andrei Malakhov's show. I'd assumed the programme was about my Mam, not about me. I said, 'I'll just sit beside you, looking pretty.' In fact, the show was a lot about me. And it was very hard. First, my so-called brother – I doubt very much if he is my brother. He'd been dragged in from God knows where to this studio, with his flowers. He gave me a letter and I said to him, 'If you're my brother, where were you when I was in the orphanage?' I'd never seen him before, all of a sudden he pops up on a TV show. I have a brother and he's called Mikey. This guy was a stranger with the title of 'brother'.

I knew I had an older sister, we found her some years ago out of the blue, but we had no idea about this guy. We look very like each other, my sister and I. She's the image of me, except older and with blonde hair. But we don't have a bond. I know where she is, that's about it. I don't feel it; if I did, I'd be in touch more.

When Malakhov showed the video of my birth mother, I found that so insulting. I thought, 'How dare you show that woman when I have a mother, right beside me?' It was horrific and cringy. Debbie is my mother, that lady had no right to be there. She's not my mother, she's a stranger who just happened to have a daughter. I thought that was very, very hurtful. I don't think Malakhov understood that. He's lovely, a sweet guy. My mam's mad about him and my family like him a lot. But that was too much.

He asked did I feel I should take care of her? Why would

he say that? It was like pulling some old woman off the street and saying, 'She's old, she made her life the way it is, now you mind her.' It was like a slap in the face. That woman made her path, she has to live it. I have a different path. She even said in the video, 'I don't have a daughter, I don't know who she is, she's just a photo.' Why would I look after someone who doesn't even know I exist? I was very quiet afterwards, I wasn't myself. A mother who didn't want me, a brother who I didn't want. It was really hard.

But that's not who I am. I have no shared history with those people, no bond, no memories. This has been a beautiful, happy story for me. My birth family doesn't have a place in that.

I think I was meant to be for the family I'm in and they were meant for me. It was so right, there were no wrongs about it. Meeting them was a fireworks-explosion moment, and when you have that moment, you know you can let your guard down, let your heart open. It was like falling in love, with a family.

APPENDIX A

The Programmes that Changed their Lives

All of our programmes were born out of the obvious needs of our children and have evolved to fill some of the biggest gaps in their lives.

Building Programme

Not all orphanages were, or are, as run down as Hortolova in 1998. We just happened to walk into one of the worst places; fate possibly. These days most are quite acceptable and even then they were nearly all better than ours.

The very first programme we started was of course the rebuilding programme. As I said earlier, rebuilding the children soon became a priority, but this story couldn't be complete without talking about the build! Back then, if you needed three cup-hooks in Russia, you had to go to three different shops. Taking on a huge institution and transforming it was a mammoth task, complicated by some of the most tedious and tangled bureaucracy you can imagine. Without the professional help and expertise of an Irish builder based in Moscow, Noel Quinn, and his excellent team, the headaches would have been considerably larger. Noel is still involved with To Russia With Love and several of our grown-up boys now work for his construction company in Moscow.

Initially, Trish, John and I attended meetings about my vision for the place. Every detail of what we wanted was described to the

Russian Department of Education, and then we would leave them to do all the drawings. Six weeks later we came back and a team of architects proudly displayed their pencil-drawn plans, the length of a kitchen table, all in minute detail. These were pre-CAD days and they had drawn every line with rulers on specialised paper. It took them weeks. We came to see where all our money was going and casually said, 'Ah, would you mind moving that up there, and this to here?' They would go pale, agree, do their utmost not to put cyanide in my tea and go back to the drawing board.

Again we arrived back, looked again and, on occasion, might decide, 'Oh dear, it was better the way it was.' More cyanide …

In fairness, they were magnificent to deal with. Initially though, they wanted to design a perfect building that the children would fit into. But I never did. I wanted the building to fit the children. I cannot count the hours we spent discussing sockets, light-fittings, taps, toilets, wardrobes, white PVC, industrial lino, door handles, fire exits, dado rails for maintenance and, of course, endless battles over the choice of paint colours. They wanted to adhere to the regulations, but I hated most of these, so I battled and battled until they gave up.

I wanted plugs in all rooms for a radio or tape-player. I didn't want flat-to-ground toilet holes, which were the norm in Russian institutions, I wanted proper toilets. I wanted mirrors everywhere as we had discovered early on that most of the children rarely saw their own reflection. I'm guessing there are architects rocking in the corner of some old folk's home now, chanting my name, and not in a good way.

The best ever was when I decided the children should be on the design team. Well, explaining that one to the department's building team was truly hilarious! The children duly attended, we examined every product, if they didn't like the Stalinesque tile samples, we changed them and we did it on a grand scale.

And so our children's home grew out of the crumbling old walls of a Dickensian orphanage. Our medical block was china blue, the beds were Ikea, quilts were 'child-friendly' – my favourite word, and one I had to explain over and over. Trish organised lovely stethoscopes for the doctor – you'd swear we'd bought her a smile.

We had photos of the children all over the walls: huge, sunny, happy, photos. Again this was born out of the sad fact that not one of them had ever seen photos of themselves before we arrived, unless they somehow had an old family album, and very few of them did. So we drowned them in photos, huge collages made by my daughter Sophie, and they adored it. In the beginning, the children stole some of the pictures of themselves to keep under pillows, but after a short time they realised they didn't need to, as the photos kept rolling in. We captured every medal, every win, every birthday, every smile, every dance class, every concert. To this day, our beautiful home is plastered in their images.

They took such pride in the building. They cleaned, tidied and wouldn't put posters on new wallpaper, although we did not mind. They snuggled up to watch TV on couches they had chosen, in rooms they had designed and kitted out. They loved it, and soon they began to love themselves.

The cleaners in the orphanage panicked endlessly at first that the children might dirty our new linos, or, God forbid, make their rooms their own, and they did exactly that. We loved it. The institution faded away and, without planning it, our de-institutionalisation programme began.

Life Skills Centre

We built a Life Skills Centre, to teach the children basic, necessary tasks. A team of Irish visited regularly with wool, material, threads, craft stuff and so on, and we funded sewing machines, even washing machines, microwaves, hobs, cookers and fridges, as orphanage children never see this kind of stuff. Using that equipment gave them really basic skills that every one of us needs and without which the world can be very daunting.

The last four Irish ambassadors to Russia have sat down in this centre and been treated to pancakes, chocolate cake, juice and tea, cooked and served by the children, all of whom – boys and girls – are encouraged to learn this from six years up. The chocolate cake class was always the most popular; I'm not sure if that's a life skill, but so what!

The staff, helped by the children, made us Russian shawls, which we all loved. They also spent hours threading tiny glass beads into bracelets. Every carer bought thousands of beads in the local market, because Russian children are brilliant at working beads. Between our knitted phone covers, our bracelets, our shawls and our hair plaits, we were soon halfway to looking Russian, which the children loved.

Sibling Trips

Our lovely sibling trips came about because we discovered after some months at Hortolova that many of our children were separated from their brothers and sisters, who were in different orphanages. So we set about the enormous task of finding each and every one of these children. The Russians didn't really understand why we were bothering, but it became very clear to us that this was the right thing to do after one of our boys, Max, called me aside one day and asked quietly was there any possibility I could locate his little sister and brother on my various visits to other orphanages. He missed them terribly and was worried about their welfare. Of course we agreed, and so the first sibling trip began.

We eventually found Max's sister and brother, although it took us over a year. We had no idea where they were, so the bus would draw up outside an orphanage and he would walk through rooms full of children, trying to search for two that looked like the children he had last seen three years previously. But eventually we found them and the reunion was highly emotional. Catya and Ura were in a huge, over-packed orphanage. Max took off his warm coat and wrapped Catya in it. He was ten, she was four. He left her with his coat. He left his boots with his little brother. We simply couldn't take them back to our orphanage, as we did not have room. Since that day we have done hundreds of trips, covered thousands of miles and reunited so many grateful children. Incidentally, I'm so proud to say Max is the first orphan to go on our board of directors. From day one he was just fantastic and never gave us any trouble – a good-hearted, intelligent, affectionate, handsome boy, who is now a fine young man. Word has it he is in love at the moment; now that's a wedding we would all hope to be at!

The Challenger Programme

I was in the Northside Partnership in Coolock one day, looking at their education programmes in Dublin for disadvantaged children and I saw something that I knew I needed to copy.

Children with potential but without adequate home resources were being put on a programme which meant more in-depth education, more extra-curricular activities, than their peers. Extra teaching aids, extra books, opportunities such as visiting universities, museums, galleries, young scientist competitions, etc., were being funded and the children were benefiting hugely. I took a copy of the programme – they were more than happy to let me plagiarise it – and we introduced it into Hortolova for our academically strongest children. It took off like wildfire. Paula O'Dwyer, one of our directors, monitored this regularly and helped choose the candidates. The children loved it and responded to it. More and more of them began reaching a higher level of education and fulfilling their potential. Every one of our children who took part in this programme went on to college or university, and the programme proved to me what I had already suspected – achievement is largely the result of opportunities and nurturing, not academic brilliance.

Mama and Baby Programmes

Mama and baby classes have been a recent addition to our programmes. We found that as some of our girls grew up and left us they would get into relationships and do all they could to please their first boyfriends. Orphan girls seek physical attention from boys and, if the boys don't want to use condoms, the girls don't make them and so they end up getting pregnant. Also, I think many of them are dying to become mothers, as they never had one. Only they have no idea what it's really like. They are unprepared, unsupported and often very young. And the fathers often don't stick around. Russian men are generally not involved in the night feeding, nappy changing, etc. All that is still considered woman's work, although these attitudes are slowly changing.

There is a very high likelihood of orphan girls putting their babies back into institutions because they have no family support and very little idea of how to cope on their own with an infant. We set up a plan to try to break this cycle. We employ nurses and other moms to help them in the first months. We buy medicine and nappies, and we fund flats so that they have somewhere to live. Igor's wife, Olga Stepanova, runs the programme. She and her team visit all of our twenty-three mums every week and teach them how to be mothers. How to bathe babies, change their nappies, play with them, feed them. We have sponsor families for some of these mothers, but we need more. We have one gorgeous Russian woman who lives in Paris now and sends in Parisian baby clothes for her sponsor baby – always sensible though, we don't need Yves Saint Laurent.

In fact the girls on this programme are doing so well that Olga has been asked by the social care department in Bryansk to mentor a full city programme for the many single moms there. We are always happy to help and pass on our wisdom. We have learned it the hard way! I love that our expertise is appreciated locally and emulated – this is thanks to the professionalism of our staff. Each one of them produces many ripples in the pond.

Socialisation Programmes

We watch our children very closely and so we see the gaps in their behaviour. We have developed many socialisation programmes to deal with these gaps and bring them closer to the experiences of children with loving, stable families. Here are just a few: birthday party programmes; ice-skating and cinema days; sports programmes – these have been hugely successful as they have such a big impact on the children's self-esteem. Bereavement counselling is regularly needed. Although it doesn't really exist in our part of Russia, we try to bring in help from other regions and outside psychologists regularly to help the children cope with the many losses in their lives. Our music classes run daily, teaching piano and accordion, as do our computer classes, although they are very low-grade, really only introductions rather than actual lessons because we cannot afford that at this point. Staff training, for every level of staff from cleaners to psychologists, is also regular.

Our playroom programme is very structured and we watch the children's development closely through play. Everything is documented and monitored, and so we pick up quickly on any extra needs or budding difficult behaviour. As soon as we spot something that requires additional input from us, we respond. Everything we do is based on raising the children's self-esteem – whether it is a day at the ice rink or extra reading lessons, the end result is the same – to bolster the children's confidence in order that they grow into stronger, less institutionalised adults. The list is therefore huge and eats up money, but the wonderful results produced by these programmes make it well worth it.

Summer Holiday Programme

For the tenth anniversary of To Russia With Love, we took 140 children to the Black Sea for two weeks, as a gift to them. They benefited so much from seeing their own beautiful country, the fresh air, freedom and space, good Russian food, and the sheer excitement of seeing the sea for the first time. Sadly, we can no longer manage luxuries like this.

Medical and Dental Programmes

These are expensive but vital; state dentist chairs are not something you would wish on your worst enemy. Zina still carries the awful memories to this day! We employ a local, private dentist and all our children visit him in town. He cleans, fills and extracts where necessary. Sadly, we can't afford braces, but he has made huge improvements. This programme costs about €5,000 a year, for one hundred children, and last year was sponsored by a generous Irish woman. We are hoping another kind benefactor will come forward this year.

Welcome Packs and Hospital Visit Programmes

On arrival, whether from home or from a previous institution, a new child feels utterly intimidated by his or her surroundings. At six years old they already know they have missed the adoption boat and so the chances are they will be in this new place until they are eighteen. It is a terrifying thought.

To minimise this, on day one we supply a welcome pack, a new schoolbag full of goodies: books, comics, stickers, football or Barbie cards. We supply fluffy pyjamas and a teddy, and the child's photo is taken and put up on the wall. They are welcomed into our family.

Orphan children regularly go to hospital, as staff can't have sick children around, and once there they never get visitors. This is because in most orphanages staff are too busy and transport is difficult. A child could be there for weeks on end, because Russians make a very big deal out of illness. At Hortolova we made the decision that our carers and staff would visit regularly with food, clean pyjamas, books and so on. Our volunteers have been doing this for years. To prevent so many going to hospital in the first place, we built a gorgeous medical block, where they can rest if they are just worn out or sad, have period pains, a sore throat or whatever. They can get into bed and just chill for a while. It's kind of a home from home – and we always pop in every time we pass to see who's in bed. The children love the chance for a little time out.

Development Plan

We have many more programmes, all built to suit individual children. And the whole thing is glued together by our 'Development Plan'. Our bible.

My 'institution guru', Derek Tracy, designed this. It came about because he used to watch us on flights, writing down everything we had to do on the backs of boarding cards, *Hello* magazine or the flyleaves of various books (the days before iPads!). And so he created this document for us. The rule is that as we walk around the orphanage, we have a responsibility to write down every promise, every maintenance issue, every request from a child, all their material needs and education issues.

Once back in Dublin, we meet, insert every single thing into our system manually and, before my next visit, it is the job of Zhenya, our Russian operations manager, to have everything done. I then bring a copy of the document and check over the list. Writing things down and putting someone's name beside each item makes things happen. It's how our wheels turn. I really need to try this at home!

If I do say so myself, we have had the happiest children's home you could ever walk into. However, it took many Irish and Russians working shoulder to shoulder. We have always tried to supply as much as a family child gets. It is not always possible and it is getting more difficult by the day due to the recession. More and more of our lovely extras have to be pared away, because we can't afford them. We are back to threadbare programmes now. Making these cutbacks is so hard, because every one of our programmes added up to brighter, stronger, happier, more confident children.

The following letter, from Olga Kurilenko, one of the first children to greet us on the day we arrived in Hortolova and a close member of the To Russia With Love family ever since, describes far better than I ever could just what these programmes have meant:

Hello, my name is Olga Kurilenko.

I would like to tell you about my life a little. It happened that my parents were deprived of parental rights, and my elder sister, my elder brother and I found ourselves in Hortolova orphanage. At that moment the living conditions in the orphanage were not very comfortable. About fifteen children were sleeping in one room and there was not enough space in this room and there were no conveniences. Our food was also not good. Everything was very old there! But the situation started changing in 2001. Everything was changing very quickly because a kind, beautiful and wonderful woman and a lot of her Irish friends appeared in the orphanage. They worked hard to improve our living conditions. New living blocks were built where four or two children could live. We had new and comfortable furniture, excellent bed-linen which was very pleasant to sleep on. Now we had playing rooms in the living blocks where we could play and watch TV, listen to music and have a rest. We felt the care of our Irish friends who surrounded us with warmth and were giving us their love, demanding nothing in stead. Now we also had sport grounds where we spent a lot of time. Irish basketball players visited us (Ed and Jerome) who taught us a lot. It was a pleasure to spend time with them. The organisation 'To Russia With Love' built us a new dining room where we could eat tasty food. A new medical block was also built where it was pleasant to go or to be ill sometimes. A new block was also built where we could cook to become prepared for independent life after school. There were also extra activities there – embroidery, knitting and sewing. I can tell you a lot about the organisation 'To Russia With Love' and about those people who gave us their warmth, care and love during many years while their own children were waiting for them in Ireland. I lived in the orphanage for eight years. And these were the best, most memorable and happiest years in my life. I had even more than the local children who lived with their parents, had, because of the Irish. I finished school in 2003 and entered a vocational school and finished it with good marks. It is very difficult to find a well-paid job in Russia. Higher education is necessary to do that. Thanks to To Russia With Love I graduated from the university in 2012 where I studied 5,5 years. Now I have got one more profession which gives me many possibilities in future. During these 5,5 years of studies the organisation 'To Russia With Love' was supporting me financially and morally. Education in Russia is expensive. I could not afford it by myself because it is very expensive. The people who help orphans are the people with big hearts. Thanks to the charity many orphans have a full-fledged and happy life.

I would like to say thanks to you on behalf of me and all those children in whose destiny you took part.

A special thanks to Igor Stepanov, his wife Olga, Evgeniy Chervonenko, Inna Konchits, Oxana, Debbie, Patricia, Dermot, Diana and many other Russian and Irish friends. I also want to say thanks to those who no longer work in the organisation but who did a lot while working.

I miss you very much! With Love and Respect to you!

Ever yours,

Olga Kurilenko

APPENDIX B

Case Studies

We have kept informal notes on all our children, for the years of their stay at Hortolova. Each volunteer added short observations during their time, to help the next team understand the children. A look through some of these notes is probably the easiest way to understand the work that To Russia With Love is doing and the challenges that our children face. These entries are a record of their circumstances, characters, progress, ambitions and achievements, small and large, throughout the years. Reading back through them always brings tears to my eyes. The improvements and successes are astounding. For reasons of privacy, some names in the case studies have been changed.

Alex Serdyukov

Mother: Mental asylum

Father: Dead, Alex doesn't know when

No brothers, no sisters

Background: Klintsy orphanage aged three, then Hortolova at six

May 2000. Visited Klintsy orphanage where he was when he was younger.

Oct. 2003. Alex has excellent English and hopes to study in Ireland next year. He is a good student and likes reading 'buy and sell' newspapers. He enjoys playing cards and sport.

Sept. 2006. On John Patchell's Leaver's Programme.

Sept. 2007. In IT college in Bryansk.

2008. Visited mother in asylum. Mother admitted with postnatal depression. Alex her first visitor in seventeen years. Very distressing situation for Alex.

2009. At university and doing well.

2011. Final year at university, studying well. Perfect English. Told his story on Malakhov show on Russian TV. Ready to spread his wings. Confident.

Sasha Ivanov

Mother: At home in Bryansk, no contact

Father: Dead

Sisters: Tamara & Vera (also in Hortolova)

Background: From home to Hortolova. Removed from mother for physical abuse, doesn't like to talk about it

Jan. 2000. Optician for glasses.

Sept. 2000. Moscow for eye treatment.

Oct. 2001. Sasha found out his father had died and went home for one night.

Nov. 2001. TB sanatorium for three months.

Oct. 2003. Very sporty, participates in all local competitions. Well-behaved, popular among children and carers. His best friend is Max. A good student, always in a good mood. Eager to learn great English. Cares for his two sisters, Tamara and Vera, also in Hortolova.

2004. Did well in final exams. Accepted onto Leaver's Programme.

2005. College studying English.

2006. College.

2007. College. Working very hard. Minds both sisters. Very responsible, excellent English, helps the Irish. Attends all To Russia With Love clinics. [To Russia With Love run weekly clinics for all children who have left, because we know they need continued support. These clinics are compulsory. We discuss every detail of each child's week, and how we can help them. We find the areas they are not coping with and try to solve these. We dole out TLC, pocket money, and tea and biscuits.]

2009–11. Moscow, works as a builder.

2011. Happy, confident. Owns an iPad. Very organised and reliable.

2012. In Moscow, living happily.

Sergey Gordeev

Mother: Lives Bryansk. Deprived of parental rights

Father: Deprived of parental rights. Whereabouts unknown

Brothers: None

Sisters: One, lives Bryansk

Background: From Bryansk shelter to Hortolova

Sept. 2003. Sergey has very serious medical problems. He has very poor sight. Severe bronchitis as he was a very heavy smoker before coming to Hortolova. Probably steals cigarettes. Smokes butts off the ground. Very small for his age. Eats badly. Delayed psychological development and needs remedial teaching. Speech defect. Well-behaved and responds well to carers' instructions.

Dec. 2003. Admitted to hospital for treatment for TB. Has a reputation for aggression and often fights with other kids in the sanatorium.

May 2004. Wears glasses and needs encouragement to do so. Worried he will be transferred to another orphanage for children with visual impairment after the summer. He is very upset by this. Going to Ireland and will have further eye treatment.

Oct. 2004. Sergey is a very happy boy and has gained a lot of confidence since the summer, due to his new 'Irish' glasses of which he is very proud. Always wears his glasses now.

July 2005. Spent two months in Ireland. Got on very well.

Jan. 2006. Went to Moscow to the oculist.

May 2007. Sergey can be hot-tempered if aggravated. He's extremely friendly, chatty and helpful with volunteers. He really loves Ireland and enjoys talking about it. He has a great sense of humour.

Aug. 2007. Still SMOKING! Still stealing cigarettes.

2008. Accordion award. Poor at school.

2009. Better behaviour, adorable. Cheeky.

2010. College.

2011. Happy. No smoking. Attends To Russia With Love clinics.

Ella Kochkaryova

Mother: An alcoholic, at home

Father: In prison for murder

Brothers: One deceased; one Bryansk orphanage; Uri, Hortolova

Sisters: One, deceased

Background: Came to Hortolova from home

May 2000. Ella witnessed her father murdering the man her mother was having an affair with. She testified at the trial against him and carries a great deal of psychological trauma. Regularly recollects her previous life with sorrow. Can suffer from bouts of depression.

June 2000. Visited Bryansk orphanage to see brother, but he had gone to the sanatorium for the summer.

June 2002. Ella is an intelligent girl and hopes to be a doctor. Likes to get extra tuition from the Irish.

Oct. 2003. Ella is good at sports. Loves to sew and attends classes in the Life Skills Centre [see Appendix A]. She is a student on the Challenger Programme [see Appendix A]. Can be aggressive at times and has trouble controlling her temper. Her behaviour has stabilised over the past two years. She appears very happy most of the time, but can get depressed.

April 2005. Excellent at volleyball. Took part in the annual regional all-orphanages competition and took first prize with the girls' team.

May 2007. For what she has been through, she's an incredibly positive girl. Very studious, athletic and popular among the other kids and all staff. Hopes to be a doctor when she leaves. A real leader. Can still have short bouts of depression.

2008. Medical College Moscow on Leaver's Programme. Working very hard. Always on Facebook. Very diligent, too hard on herself. Suffers with headaches from over-study and Moscow life. Worries about small brother, Uri, whom she is devoted to.

2009. Father released from prison. Ella met him initially and helped him with food and clothing but has minimal communication now. Many Irish friends, attached to sponsor family. Mother requests money for alcohol. Ella continually says no.

2009–11. College, Moscow. Studying. Boyfriend. Happy.

ACKNOWLEDGEMENTS

It is hard to pick out names from all the many who shared our miles, tears and workload. Please forgive me for those I have omitted.

Ann and Katie Delaney – for all the love, support and friendship. For naming the charity. Ann we miss you terribly.

Julie Hogan and Joanna Fortune – the brains behind me.

Anne Harris, Aengus Fanning and the *Sunday Independent* – for their years of support and advice. Aengus is sadly missed.

Alice Williams – a very special lady, a fighter, a giver, a mountain climber, an elf.

Ann Norton and Laura Dowdall – forensic penny counters.

Eddie Kane and all the SuperValu stores and staff – for their support, fund-raising and our boardroom.

Laura Collins and family – for the trust, support and special moments in Dublin, Russia and San Francisco.

Joe Duffy – supporter, an endorser, the man behind the Beslan project.

Sandbar, Tibors, Hemmingways, Bay, Kinara and Moloughneys; the Clontarf restaurants – for feeding my family when I was with my Russian kids and all the fund-raising.

Larry Sheerin – for all his kindness to our boys, a great daddy to many.

Angela Kelly – for endless hours doing the books, banking, walking; the perfect volunteer.

Gerry McCarthy – for the support, the connections, the friendship, the 'challenging' emails!

Marie Cregan – for the support and advice.

Ronan Murtagh – for using his Citation X Jet as a shelf for our charity brochure.

The Paddy Gang in Moscow – for all they have done, they know who they are. Thank you.

Marian Keyes – for her love, her tears, her kindness, her generosity and her foreword. And to Tony for looking after her when the tears started.

Matt and Jackie Donoghue – for their support and kindness; Jackie is missed by us all.

Rory McDyer – for giving us our first office.

Neil O'Brien – adviser, friend, life coach.

Mary Kennedy – for her support, advice and friendship.

Pat Kenny – TV host, started the snowball rolling down the hill.

Gay Byrne – for his time and support.

Nicola, Lucianne, Annette, Ann, Olga, Amy, Cassandra and Louise – for making life easy for us in the Dublin office.

Clodagh Grealy and her parachutists – for risking their lives for our children!

Natasha Bersegian and KFC – for their support.

Marie Hunt – for all the support in Dublin and for giving us one less to mind.

Tamara Starshinka – for mopping up my tears and calming me down; her support as deputy governor was invaluable.

Sean McCusker – for his kindness.

Neven Maguire – for his kindness and his cooking.

Kamal Boushi – for his advice and support.

Irina Nemchinova – wonderful social worker, fighter and defender of many of our children.

Tommy Tiernan – for his time and Winnebago!

Jeannette Byrne – for all her support and her very special CD.

Dave Conachy – for airbrushing me, making me look thinner and gorgeous, and more importantly his time, care and stunning images of our children.

The administration of Bryansk – for treating me like one of their own.

The governor and administration of Kaluga – for their welcome and support.

The wonderful staff of Hortolova orphanage – for doing their best every day with our children, they need a pay rise.

Rehab – for my wonderful award; but really a thousand of us should have collected it, not just me.

All the friends of my own three children – for working at every ball, supermarket collection and all other mad events we had. You were super and always looked stunning!

Roly Saul – for his kindness.

Anna Grenfell – for her connections and support.

Tom Byrne, his family, all his artist friends – for their support. If only all fund-raising could be that easy …

Lev – my friend, midnight rescuer and bodyguard whenever I needed one. If ever a James Bond movie needs an extra …

The corporates in Russia who are slowly beginning to help.

The management and staff of Kellogg's – for their cake sales, scholarship programme and support in both Ireland and Russia.

Kupi VIP who gave me hope that Russians would help.

The Russian community in Ireland – for trusting and supporting us.

Andrei Malakhov – for being a friend and using his celebrity to highlight our plight.

Peter Gannon – a donor, a friend, a wonderful young man. From all the children in 'Gannon Hall', thank you.

Richard and Paul Nolan – for their support.

The host families who took in our children when they needed homes.

Norah Casey – for all her support for me over the years.

Keith Duffy – eye candy, friend, and I'm thrilled to say I have slept with him, if bunk beds with four others squashed into one train carriage, counts; a great ambassador for autism and buyer of our children's plasma TV.

The wonderful people of Loughrea – for all their fund-raising.

Richard Hannaford – for his kindness; he is sadly missed.

Sean Boland – our own Michael Bublé, friend, trainer, fund-raiser, cleaner of many toilets.

All staff and inmates of Wheatfield Prison – for making so much happen.

Every Elf – for wearing hats and aprons and singing carols endlessly, sprinkling their magic and putting smiles on faces that sometimes forgot how to smile.

Every person that gave days, weeks, months, too many to mention. Here are just a handful of names from the huge files of people that went out: Deirdre Davies, Lavinia Mossop, Maedhbh Nic Dhonnchadha, Eileen Kirby, Sheila McSweeney, Paul Longmore – only some of an endless, endless list.

Dr Hampson – for her kindness and support, and allowing me to always jump the queue.

Angela Smith, Margaret Bowman and all the foster experts – for their support and for their training.

The Department of Foreign Affairs in Ireland – for their years of support.

Pat Byrne – for helping me get the weight off and then watching me put it back on.

Paul and Maria Quinn – for all their time, care and support and map reading and many summits.

Sasha Chernukin – gorgeous, professional, kind, project management second to none, sadly missed.

The Irish ambassadors who have visited our children, and their wonderful staff in Moscow.

The Russian ambassadors in Dublin who have supported everything we do, and all their kind staff.

Pauline Bewick – for the wonderful supply of art, auctioned over many years.

Brian Britton – for his wisdom.

Sarah Caden – generous supporter, who looks beautiful standing beside Brendan O'Connor at every gig.

Brendan Magonnel – for his generosity and continuous acknowledgement that Russians changed the course of history during the Second World War.

My board of directors who guide me, mind me, advise me, support me, fund-raise for the children and govern with kindness and a rod of iron.

Diana Hurley, Carmel McConnell and her dad – for the endless gathering, fund-raising, singing, support.

Barry Fitzpatrick – for his support.

Lord Mayor Eibhlin Byrne and Lord Mayor Gerry Breen – for their support and friendship.

Brian Hughes – a friend, loyal supporter and 'struggling' but fantastic hotelier, who always says nice things about me and finally gave me that Irish dancing medal last year, thank God!

Brian Mathews – friend, supporter, elf and a wonderful liar for telling me I looked great during the 'burnout'.

A special thanks to Emily Hourican – for listening to my outpourings for months and finally moulding it all into a lovely shape that we can all be proud of. A very patient, sweet, gorgeous, tadpole-hating, new member of the To Russia With Love family.

Oprah Winfrey – for 'speckled puppies' and teaching me a very valuable lesson – that by telling someone they are beautiful, no matter what they look like, they will begin to believe it. God bless the days when I actually was a 'Clontarf housewife' and watched her every afternoon.

Cyclone Couriers – for all the speed, efficiency and generosity.

Phonovation and the mobile networks – for their contribution to our fund-raising efforts.

Simon Bell – our youngest ever fund-raiser and member of the X Factor Club.

Another Avenue and Windmill Lane – for the many hours spent cutting and editing footage and helping us tell our story.

Every ball ticket buyer, every lady who lunched, every golf classic supporter, every keyring buyer, every text message sender, every mini-marathon and marathon runner, every Darling who Dined, every large donor for the enormous difference they made. Every corporate that allowed us access to their CSR Policy, every child that drops pocket money or cake sale money to our office, every walker who circled the globe for us and every mountain climber that cursed us as they crawled up Kilimanjaro, Machu Picchu, the Great Wall and the Pyramids. Every Christmas gift purchaser, every carol singer, every family, individual and couple that contributes by standing order and direct debit, every celebrity who took part in the Concert Hall success, every school that has fund-raised.

The people of my beautiful little country. I cannot thank you enough for your generosity to us and the children we care for. We cannot continue without your support. Please donate what you can to help us continue the minding. They need us still.

All the children in To Russia With Love. There are no words to thank you for allowing us to be a part of your lives. We love you, you have stolen our hearts. I hope we can continue this magical journey we are on with you until you no longer need us.

And if The Academy ever read the above it will seriously hamper my chances of an Oscar!